Lefty's Playbook

What the Left Does Not Want You to Know

WestBow
PRESS

WestBow Press books may be ordered through booksellers or by contacting:

WestBow Press
A Division of Thomas Nelson
1663 Liberty Drive
Bloomington, IN 47403
www.westbowpress.com
1-(866) 928-1240

ISBN: 978-1-4497-0240-3 (sc)
ISBN: 978-1-4497-0241-0 (hc)
ISBN: 978-1-4497-0239-7 (e)

Library of Congress Control Number: 2010934552

Printed in the United States of America

WestBow Press rev. date: 12/07/2010

Dedicated to all patriots, past and present.

Contents

Preface

This book is about Lefty—better known as the political *left*, the force in global politics that seeks to counteract the political *right*. But to just simply say "the political *left*" is a gross oversimplification of a complex philosophy that has existed since the beginning of time and unfortunately, will exist as long as humanity exists. Due to this ubiquitous occurrence in time and space, those of us who cherish liberty must equip ourselves to understand its nature, just like we would any chronic medical condition. Consequently, once we understand it, we can then learn to manage it in order to maintain a healthy and viable culture.

This book is intended to be an introduction *to understanding leftism*. To chronicle all the left has done and is doing would require an encyclopedic undertaking. The tactics and methods of the left are too immense and complex to condense into a simple volume. With this in mind, the primary goal of *Lefty's Playbook* is to expose the basics of leftist thought and activity. For some, this book is intended to be in part educational. For others, this book may be confirmation of what they have suspected all along—there is a force that seeks to impose its political will on the rest of the world, a force bent on acquiring power, operating methodically and persistently toward that goal; that force is known as the left.

The Game

"Freedom is not free."

—**Korean War Veteran Memorial**

One can only imagine the intense emotional stress experienced by Peter Fechter as he prepared for his imminent escape. After all, failure was not an option. Even though his existence was miserable before, the punishment that would follow if he were captured would be tremendously worse. And even worse than that, he could be wounded in the process and still end up captured. To add to the sum of fears, the guards were not known for their humane treatment of prisoners attempting escape. Their cold manner and complete lack of empathy was reinforced by their reputation. The guards would just as soon shoot at an escapee as they would a clay pigeon.

Yet, conversely, to Peter, the thought of freedom edged out the thoughts of injury, punishment, and even death. To stay was to remain in perpetual misery; to escape was to taste freedom, even if temporary. It is perhaps with these thoughts in mind that Peter and a fellow prisoner, as they were hiding out in a carpentry workshop near the prison wall, waited for the optimal moment to begin their mad dash to freedom. In what must have been an emotional waterfall of intense self-examination and desperation of unimaginable proportions, they jumped out of a window and ran across the so-called death-strip (a strip running between the main prison wall and a parallel fence). Then came the crucial moment: climbing over a wall of concrete and barbed wire. With this last rite of passage also came visibility, which in turn would assuredly draw gunfire from the guards, whose willingness to maim or kill was based on fact, not legend.

Although his comrade, in desperation, succeeded in making it over the wall, Peter, still on the wall, was shot in the pelvis. In a moment of shock and horror, Peter fell back into the abyss he was desperately trying to escape. Despite his screams, he received no assistance. In fact, no one came to help him, most likely for fear of how the guards would react. Within an hour, Peter Fechter bled to death right where he fell, just a few yards from the freedom he had envisioned.

This was the price of *Republikflucht*. The year was 1963. The "prison" was the infamous (now defunct) country of East Germany. The "prison wall" was the notorious Berlin Wall. "Republikflucht" (English translation: "fleeing the country") was the criminal charge faced by East German citizens who were caught *fleeing the country*. Yes, you are reading that correctly: *fleeing the country*.

Formally implemented in 1957, the charge of *Republikflucht* provided up to three years in prison for attempting to escape from East Germany, while even more severe penalties were applied to border guards who attempted to escape. Just assisting an escape from East Germany could land a person in prison for up to two years. Yet despite the potential for punishment, from 1957 until the fall of the East German regime, more than seventy-five thousand East German citizens and fifty-five hundred border guards were imprisoned for attempting *Republikflucht*. Of these, it is estimated that more than five thousand people tried to escape by climbing over the Berlin Wall, of which approximately one hundred died in the process of grasping for liberty, most of who were shot to death.

Because of its symbolic nature, escaping by climbing over the Berlin Wall received the lion's share of attention. However, there were other methods and border regions that inspired *Republikflucht*. Some escaped to the West by tunnels, stowing away in cargo and even hot-air balloons. Some disguised themselves as soldiers while others made spontaneous escapes after observing security lapses along the East German border. Escapes and escape attempts occurred all along the East German border, including the Baltic Sea.

Some were successful and some were not. Some were gunned down by border guards; others were killed by land mines, while others drowned in rivers or the open sea. All told, almost a thousand people died trying to escape East Germany.[1]

In reality, what these "escapees" were guilty of was yearning for freedom, and consequently, fleeing the tyranny of Socialism. They were human beings with an inner spark of independence driven to escape, even with the knowledge that the potential outcomes were incarceration, harsh treatment, and even death. Ultimately, these virtual inmates were not just breaking out of a communist country or fleeing an oppressive regime; they were escaping an ideological prison run by a warden whose name is *Lefty*.

Lefty: An Introduction

Lefty who? With the *perceived* absence in modern times of the infamous dictators of old, one may consider Lefty, better known as the political left, to be the embodiment of the historical or contemporary sociopolitical complex known as the left. In short, Lefty is the personification of leftist ideology.

Although some may believe that leftist ideology only thrives in specific regions of the world, a closer inspection would show that the left is a force on every continent and in virtually every country—strong in some and weak in others. Likewise, a historical inspection of the near and ancient past would reveal that the left has existed throughout all time. Based on this assessment, coupled with history's rearview evidence, the projection can easily be made that the left will, in all probability, exist as long as humankind walks the earth. Once accepting the idea that the left is an unavoidable condition of life, we must first learn how to identify it and second, how to deal

---

1   Compiled from the following: http://www.grenzer.com/, http://www.berlinwall.itgo.com/climb.htm, and http://en.wikipedia.org/wiki/Peter_Fechter.

with it, lest we end up in the predicament that Peter Fetcher and millions of others have found themselves.

But how does one identify or distill the essence of the left? After considerable observation, one will notice time and time again a recurring underlying theme in all leftist activity. And no, it is not a better world with all of its trappings; quite the contrary. *The common denominator in all leftist movements past and present is simply this: **the desire for complete power and control**—and just as important, not only the desire to have it and at some point return it or lose it but to have it **in perpetuity.***

Now, with the primal character trait of the left exposed, the persona of the left is made substantially easier to recognize. The left can therefore be defined as any person, group, or movement, contemporaneous or historical, which has coveted *the desire for complete power and control, in perpetuity.*

Furthermore, this leftist amalgamation can be expanded to include special interests (persons, groups, and movements) that may not ultimately desire raw political power but need that power for one simple reason: because their special ideology, belief, or practice runs cross-current to common sense and or cultural values. As a result, political enforcement is the only remaining avenue for their niche agenda to be imposed upon a free society. In this case, such entities are equivalent to the power-mad lefties, since they symbiotically assist and bolster the left. It is the classical case of one hand washing the other. In the mind of the naïve special interest protagonist, the outcome they desire is achieved in exchange for supporting the left's acquisition of power. As we shall see, however, this relationship will most likely terminate as soon as Lefty reaches the goal, at which point the *special interest* will no longer be *special* or even tolerated!

But changing a culture and garnering such power does not come easy. For the left to gain political power, individual liberties must be wrested from the populace at large. And of course, as it is with human nature, individual liberties are not easily given up or taken away. One must be forced, coerced, manipulated, or deceived in some manner. Thus the left, by scheming to use force, coercion, manipulation, and deception, combined with free societies' open-door policy to contrarian ideologies, sets its sights on seizing the mantle of power.

It is quite unfortunate that the Achilles' heel of democracy can be the very freedoms that make it a democracy. For a true democracy to exist, it must allow for leftist elements to freely express their bankrupt ideology. Otherwise, without freedom of expression, the democracy is akin to a leftist entity! Because of this paradox, traces of the left exist within free societies the world over. Yet it is from fledgling bases of operation that the left has proven time and time again to be successful in spreading its destructive ideology.

Through the use of the left's innate skill sets of deceit and trickery, the left markets its madness in the form of carefully crafted slogans, speeches, and writings, also known as propaganda, to lull the societal Goliath to sleep. Then, once the society is drugged into a political slumber (usually accompanied by an *engineered* moral tailspin), leftist elements do their part to ensure that the decline continues. At the same time, the left laboriously shores up influential positions in the societal framework, preparing for that long-awaited moment when message and movement can be dictated by the leftist powers in place. Interestingly, the leftist's takeover of society employs a technique observed in nature.

In a parasitic manner, the left attaches itself (joins, hires on, enlists in—think infiltration) to hosts (government, media, business, etc.—established organizations) and through time and effort, slowly digests each host, one by one. Toward the end of the process, the hosts are virtually enveloped by the parasites; what was once a collection of viable hosts becomes a collection of life-draining parasites. Then, on cue, with all the levers having been wrested from the old order, a new order is rapidly ushered in. In the final stages, intimidation and force, legal and otherwise, is the leftist method of choice to overthrow and seal the fate of a once-free people. Once the left has won and the game is over, more intimidation, backed up by force, including imprisonment and extermination, is used to keep the societal Goliath from ever rising again.

The process just described is a well thought out plan that does not come easy, but such an overwhelming task does not deter Lefty.

While most in society are happy to enjoy life, family, friends, sports, weekend barbecues, etc., Lefty is obsessively focused on ascending to the heights of power, always thinking, always scheming, *always.* Sound paranoid? Skeptics and truth-deflecting leftists can file the next bit of information under the category, "While You Were Sleeping."

The following is excerpted from a transcript of an interview conducted in the 1980s with Yuri Bezmenov, a former KGB operative who defected to the West in 1970. Born the son of a high-ranking Soviet Army officer, his pedigree naturally made him a de facto member of the Communist Party. Consequently, being a "party member" provided access to the "good" life in the Soviet Union, which included elite schools inside the Soviet Union—schools that turned out the finest in dedicated communists. Doing his duty for the motherland, Mr. Bezmenov became an expert in Indian culture and Indian languages and was eventually assigned by the KGB to India, which, incidentally, is where he defected. On the topic of *ideological subversion,* Mr. Bezmenov had this to say:

> *"It has nothing to do with espionage. I know that espionage intelligence gathering looks more romantic ... But in reality the main emphasis of the KGB is NOT in the area of intelligence at all. According to my opinion, and the opinions of many defectors of my caliber, only about 15 percent of time, money, and manpower is spent on espionage as such. The other 85 percent is a slow process which we call ideological subversion, active measures, or psychological warfare. What it basically means is: to change the perception of reality of every American that despite of the abundance of information no one is able to come to sensible conclusions in the interest of defending themselves, their families, their community, and their country. It's a great brainwashing process which goes very slow ... Most of the activity of the department [KGB] was to compile huge amount volume of information, on individuals who were instrumental in creating public opinion. Publisher, editors, journalists, uh actors, educationalists, professors of political science. Members of parliament, representatives of business circles. Most of these*

people were divided roughly into two groups: those who would tow the Soviet foreign policy, they would be promoted to positions of power through media and public manipulation; [and] those who refuse the Soviet influence in their own country would be character assassinated OR executed physically, come Revolution."

After explaining how it is done, Mr. Bezmenov went on to provide a real-world scenario:

"Same way as in a small town of Hua in South Vietnam; several thousands of Vietnamese were executed in one night when the city was captured by [the] Viet Cong for only two days; and American CIA could never figure out— how could [the communists] possibly know each individual, where he lives, where to get him; and [in order that they] would be arrested in one night basically in four hours before dawn, put on a van, driven out of the city limits and shot. The answer is very simple. Long before communists occupy the city, there was extensive network of informers; local Vietnamese citizens who knew absolutely everything about people who are instrumental in public opinion—including barbers and taxi drivers. Everyone who was sympathetic to United States was executed. Same thing was done under the guidance of the Soviet Embassy in Hanoi, and same thing I was doing in New Delhi. To my horror, I discovered that in the files were people who were doomed to execution. There were names of pro-Soviet journalists, with whom I was personally friendly." [2]

Many other former Marxists (leftists) have admitted a similar story: given the assignment from on high, they endeavored to stealthily and relentlessly recruit indigenous operatives and till the native political soil with leftist principles and proxies.

Although the left is "shy" to admit it, there are plans as well as a standard operating procedure—a playbook, if you will—that is well understood by the leftist faithful, a playbook for and by the left that is unavailable for the public at large, at least in a comprehensive and

---

2   http://www.freerepublic.com/focus/f-news/2095202/posts.

abridged form. Not to say that volumes of works on leftist subversion do not exist; one cannot ignore reference material from such leftist hall of fame authors such as Karl Marx. Yet it would appear that the entire volume of leftist tactics and aims remains unbounded or at the very least, hard to find.

There are two main reasons why this playbook has been kept under wraps, and for good reason. First, once a nonconformist understands the playbook, spotting the leftist for the radical he or she is, becomes easier. Second, once the public at large understands what the real game plan is, Lefty's ascent to power is made much more difficult or possibly, impossible!

So how do we know that a playbook exists? A playbook is nothing more than a collection of predetermined patterns of action or behavior. And wherever leftists are, regardless of time and space, they engage in the same actions and behavioral patterns over and over; they operate as if guided by a playbook.

It is important to note that this playbook of the left is not a perfect operations manual, for the imperfection and invariability of humankind prevents perfect execution. Rather, it is, as leftists like to say, a "living document" with new tactics and plays added as Lefty adapts to new situations. Fortunately for humanity, Lefty has one major inescapable character flaw: he (or "she"; "he" will frequently be used only for simplicity) can never be honest about his ultimate plans. Thus, he can never speak consistently or truthfully about his wild-eyed aims while going about his deceit. Because of this, he must constantly refer to the playbook on how to respond, react, and obfuscate.

Based on what has been discussed so far, being a leftist sounds like a horrible existence, *n'est pas*? To appreciate what would drive an individual into such a demented state, it is important to understand the psyche of the left, to understand how the real leftists think.

Basically, leftists are the ultimate in control freaks. When it comes to control, leftists not only desire to control the actions of others (key word, *others*), but also desire to control the thoughts of others (key word, *others*). Yes, that's correct: the ultimate nirvana for a leftist is to control your thoughts. The idea itself has been known to make leftists salivate uncontrollably. However, should they have to settle for something less, say perhaps some sub-celestial earthly gains like good, old-fashioned tyrannical rule, they will be more than able to cope.

But are all leftists that insane? Looking from the outside in, the worshippers that find solace in the church of the Left may appear to consist of many denominations: liberalism, progressivism, socialism, National Socialism, fascism, Marxism, communism, and totalitarianism—just to name the ones that come to mind! To the disinterested casual observer, some leftist "denominations" may seem to be innocuous when compared to others, such as when comparing liberalism to fascism. Yet in the final analysis, these denominational labels appear to distinguish nothing. Rather, such masquerading labels' only purpose is to act as placating agents. Their only purpose is to satisfy the current level of cultural tolerance toward leftist ideology. That is to say, in a relatively free society, leftists are called liberals; in a society of lesser freedoms, leftists are called socialists; in a society of even lesser freedoms, leftists are called fascists; in a society of even lesser freedoms, leftists are called communists.

This underlying principle is one that the left desperately does not want to be understood—namely, that there is scarcely a difference between a liberal, a socialist, a fascist, a communist, or a dictator. Either one graduates to the next level or one enables those headed leftward. The difference that remains between the monikers is that it is only the acquisition of power that distinguishes a liberal, a socialist, a fascist, a communist, and a dictator. That is to say, a socialist is only a liberal who has obtained more power; a fascist is only a socialist who has obtained more power; a communist is only a fascist who has obtained more power; and a dictator is only a communist who has consolidated power. In summation, the ultimate leftist is the ultimate dictator; is the ultimate communist; is the ultimate fascist; is the ultimate socialist; is the ultimate liberal.

Anatomy of a Maniac

Using history as a guide, it soon becomes evident that leftists are a collection of the deranged and or wounded child, the latter seeming to be the most prevalent. Interestingly, a great number of leftists of all stripes seem to have some unmet childhood need that is carried unresolved on into adulthood and throughout their entire lives. Now we know that this is the case in some measure with a great number of us: no path of life is perfect and most of us bear some stripes from our childhood—some minor, some major. With a leftist, however, the problem is so magnified to the degree that when the leftist reaches maturity and garners political power, society is unwillingly enveloped into a massive group therapy experiment, of which, under most circumstances, the public is never made aware!

Think about it. Not only is the public not typically aware of leftists' true reasons for wanting to "serve" the public, but the public is also not typically aware of the actual psychosis behind the "public servant's" actions. Even an experienced counselor may take months to peel back the layers of the counselee to find out the root causes of his or her behavioral issues. But in the case of leftist political figures, they do their best to mask who they really are, not to mention masking their true intentions and design for society. It is even scarier to think that they themselves may not even know what drives them. For some, all they may know is that they are automatically driven to do what they do. This does not excuse them, however, for by the time they begin to covet power, they well understand the difference between right and wrong. When it comes to their lust for power and control, they simply choose to do wrong.

Correspondingly, to what extent leftists are driven is determined by how deep and reinforced their psychological scars are. Thus, axiomatically, the deeper the psychosis, the more havoc they will wreak on society when given the reigns of power. The old saying, "Misery loves company" rings true in this sense, because once in power, a leftist wants everyone else to experience the same pain he or she has experienced. The more pain the leftist experienced, or *thinks* he or she experienced, the more pain he or she believes society should experience.

In contrast to any scarring in their early emotional development, derangement is another factor that has thrown many an individual into rabid mental hysteria and consequentially, to the left side. Leftist derangement seems to come about in different ways. First, it can happen in a deliberate method, where the blank slate of the child is exploited by a leftist to suit the needs of the movement—which is why the education system is heavily infiltrated and manipulated. Second, it can happen by virtual osmosis, through an upbringing in an abnormal environment. For example, some children of dictators have been known to grow up to be more ruthless and insane than their progenitors. Third, in what can be considered happenstance, derangement can stem from traumatic occurrences that occurred during childhood or adolescence. For these types, it appears that at some point in the developmental stage, a mental "switch" is flipped to a defective position. From that point on they see life through a distorted prism. The cause may be attributed to some sudden physiological change, a traumatic or series of traumatic events, a negative influence at a crucial developmental stage, and so on.

For those of us on the outside looking in, determining when one changes from a member of society to a menace to society is difficult. For a leftist, psychological degradation could have begun in childhood or even happen in the process of obtaining power. It could very well be that the mania starts when the leftist experiences his or her first real taste of political power—a combination that has proven to generate a potion that is spellbinding.

Regardless of when and how, once induced, the arena of the leftist is a treacherous environment—an environment that naturally contributes to further devolution of the soul. As leftist power increases, so does the need to retain it, and so does the need to protect against the loss of power. In such a case, the frantic leftist will rise to ever-increasing measures to ensure the retention of power. In turn, paranoia and its derivatives accompany the downward spiral into the mental abyss. Interestingly enough, the paranoia is well-founded since leftists realize that there are other power-seeking control freaks just like themselves!

One noticeable side effect of leftist mental demise is, among others, projection. That is, negative psychological traits that run deep in Lefty's psyche are conveniently applied to the opposition. It has a twofold purpose: primarily to put Lefty's own crazed conscience at ease, and secondarily, to deflect away from the leftist and generate angst toward the opposition. Quite often, whatever a leftist accuses the opposition of perpetrating, you can bet that the leftist is infinitely guiltier, in spades.

As it turns out, projection just happens to be a convenient psychosis for a leftist. First, a leftist does not want him or herself or anyone else to critically think about who he or she is or what he or she is up to. Second, a leftist does not want society to critically think about important issues and actually viable solutions, for a leftist only wants people to *feel* about issues and despise and fear the opposition. Thus, the leftist's whole existence can be summed up in two words: feeling and fear. The problem for the rest of us is that Lefty has deceived himself into thinking that he cannot release his fear and feel at one with his world until he has total and complete control over ours.

So what kind of real-world environments have bred such a psychosis? While reading the following examples, understand that these excerpts are simply a small biographical slice of their lives, yet a very significant and telling one (name appears first, in bold).

"Zey":

"… had been regularly whipped by his father … but he hardly ever admitted the full extent of the rage he must have felt for his own father, a very severe teacher who had tried through beatings to 'make a man' out of his son." [3]

"Soso":

"There were dreadful scenes … 'One day when his father was drunk he picked him up and threw him violently to the floor. There was blood in the boy's urine for days afterwards.' The big fistfights with no holds barred—that was what little Soso saw from the day he was born." [4]

---

3   http://www.vachss.com/guest_dispatches/alice_miller2.html
4   Edvard Radzinsky, *Stalin: the first in-depth biography based on explosive new documents from Russia's secret archives*, New York: Anchor Books, 1997, p 24.

"Adi":

> *"'If there were ever quarrel[s] or differences of opinions between my parents,' she continued 'it was always on account of the children. It was especially my brother ... who challenged my father to extreme harshness and who got his sound thrashing every day ...' His poor beloved mother, he used to remark, to whom he was so attached, lived in constant concern about the beatings he had to take, sometimes waiting outside the door as he was thrashed."* [5]

Given the natural innocence of children and how devastating such treatment can be, it makes one wonder how it can ever be tolerated. The miserable upbringing these little children had to endure is heartbreaking. The lifelong pain they endured one can only imagine. Their childhoods permanently scarred them as they had their empathy and innocence literally beaten straight out of them.

Yet the plight of these children was not lost in statistics. These were not just any little boys of any consequence; their lives influenced the world over. *Zey* grew up to be known as Mao Zedong, to whose existence an estimated 55 million deaths are attributed. *Soso* grew up to be known as Josef Stalin, to whose existence an estimated 50 million deaths are attributed. *Adi* grew up to be known as Adolf Hitler, to whose existence an estimated 42 million deaths are attributed.[6] And if these unfathomable statistics are not enough, such atrocities do not include the untold misery and despair hoisted upon those who survived. The lesson is clear: a traumatic childhood can have tremendous implications for the world.

A similar review of other infamous tyrants will generally lead to a similar result. Most of them came from scarred beginnings and carried their emotional wounds into adulthood. Some, at one point in their trek to power, spent time under confinement in either jail or house arrest. And believe it or not, at one time or another, some were considered to be of no consequence. But make no mistake, the seemingly insignificant liberal, socialist, or fascist spouting off ridiculous philosophies today has

5   Ian Kershark, *Hitler, 1889-1936: hubris*, New York: W.W. & Company, Inc., 1999, p.13

6   http://users.erols.com/mwhite28/warstat1.htm.

all the potential to be the "great leader" of tomorrow and in most cases, were yesterday's abused and neglected child.

It should be noted that not all leftists rise to the position of national dictator. Some are content to work in the background, manipulating incognito. It is also important to note that the trauma does not have to be so drastic to cause one to gravitate to leftist ideology. Psychological trauma can be a matter of degrees. Childhood scars can take many forms and do not necessarily entail physical abuse. They can, for example, be in the form of abandonment, neglect, or emotional abuse. We all live in our own existence: what feels bad for one is still bad to the individual, and how that influences one's outlook in life matters and colors the world as one sees it. On the other hand, there are those who had scarred beginnings but were able to overcome the dark side.

The problem with leftists is that they take their mangled emotions and force society to participate in their twisted method of group therapy—a price millions upon millions have unwillingly paid. Society should always be on guard for such an individual and heed the warnings from history. ***Caveat civis!*** *Beware of the wounded child that wants to lead you.*

The Faithful

"It is hard to free fools from the chains they revere."
—Voltaire

Followers enable leaders. Clearly, self-appointed leftist tyrants would be nonentities if it were not for the misguided followers. Is it not confounding and simultaneously depressing to think that someone would actually follow and support such an animal? One must ask oneself, "What kind of person falls for this twisted ideology?"

It would seem that such individuals could be easily categorized, but the reality is that the gamut of leftist followers does not fit into one convenient description. They exist throughout the entire spectrum of society, without regard to income, education, or religion, ranging from the reluctant to the rabid, from the duped to the devoted. Do not be conformed into thinking that every leftist supporter wears a beret and spouts off slogans heralding the rights of the proletariat while snarling at the "evils" of the bourgeois class. The fact of the matter is that leftists come from all walks of life, rich and poor, young and old, educated and uneducated, and so on and so on.

On the other hand, there is evidence that certain socioeconomic profiles have a history of supporting the left more often than not. Take unions, for example. Because union leadership tends to be infiltrated by leftist handmaidens, union members generally tend to support leftists simply because they are influenced and swayed by the union leadership. Likewise, the poor, constantly being fed the empty promises of leftist propaganda by self-appointed representatives, also generally tend to support the leftists. But just because members of these "constituencies" support the left doesn't mean they believe in core leftist principles. On the contrary, should the truth become known, most would probably withdraw support in an instant.

In light of the last sentence, some clarification concerning generalizations is necessary before moving on. Generalizations are just what the definition implies: a premise that is somewhere in the high percentages yet never reaching complete inclusion and, of course, never infallible. For example, it is well understood that there are union members or financially impoverished individuals who are conservative, love their country, and are just as upset with the left as anyone else. But such individuals do not *generally* control and operate the radical leadership within their respective groups. Rather, it is those who lead the group who, in wanting to please their leftist masters and or satisfy personal wants, do their utmost to control, influence, and speak for the groups they claim to represent. And even though the leadership does not necessarily control all of those who belong to the group, having a platform within the group nonetheless provides a sustainable vehicle for captive education and direction.

Now, with that in mind, let's explore the different types of followers who knowingly *or unknowingly* assist Lefty in his plans to undermine society.

The Uniformed

This gaggle consists of that vast swath of the public who have no interest in politics or government. They typically want to just live their lives and do not interact much with political systems. Along comes a message that sounds reasonable and perhaps offers them a better standing in life. Without care or concern, they accept the messenger and message at face value. Because they are not looking for subterfuge, they do not find it. They are too involved in living life to spend time dissecting political players. And quite frankly, they do not want to. And in a way, who can blame them?

However, in a true republic, it is not a question of whether one should or shouldn't have to keep an eye on the political arena. There is little choice if one wants to retain one's liberties. In order to maintain a strong republic, it is imperative that the electorate be engaged and informed. This is the very reason why referendums such as term limits are poor remedies when compared against an engaged and informed electorate. In a vibrant republic, the greatest term limit procedure is done at the ballot box, whereas countless referendums are actually signs of a political system in trouble. When true statesmanship is in charge of the government, referendums are virtually unnecessary. Thomas Jefferson best summed up this concept: "The price of freedom is eternal vigilance."

The Dependent

Having a dependent electorate is exactly what the left wants. To accomplish this, the left uses whatever distractions necessary to keep the masses mired in misery and focusing on something other than the bigger picture. One of the greatest tactics is to keep individuals occupied with their own problems. It is a well-known psychological fact that well-adjusted individuals are able to focus beyond themselves and impact the world around them in a positive manner. In contrast, someone with personal problems (guilt, addictions, etc.) will have a greater difficulty seeing beyond themselves and helping themselves, never mind helping others. Such individuals usually need to heal first before they can reach out beyond their own personal horizon. Such individuals will also more readily turn to outside help. Consequently, Lefty, in the form of a political party, is more than willing to be their personal "savior."

As far as the left is concerned, the more inner-focused, brooding victims we have in society the better. How is this accomplished? By promoting self-destructive ideas such as narcotic usage, promiscuity, and pornography, just to name a few, all of which leave a wake of victims in their path. And of course, the left loves victims—a constituency that leftists are more than happy to assist in swelling the ranks.

The Emotional

This gaggle is comprised of those caught up in the emotion of the propaganda. These types typically haven't really thought about what is said, they just know that they feel good about *what* is being said. This is different than the uninformed; this type of follower may read books by the propagandists, attend speeches, and donate to pet causes. They are emotionally swept off their feet and are easy to spot. Ask them about policy details and they will quickly dispel any notion of having made an informed decision. Typically, they regurgitate whatever emotional appeal has been made to them. If the propagandist states that he wants to bring people together, they will respond with, "He will bring people together!" These are the *Stepford* followers. Fueled on only by an emotional basis, they walk around in an intellectual coma, supporting, or better said, hypnotically abetting the leftist leader.

The Loyalists

There are those who simply follow a political party based on their family's allegiance. This trans-generational political gene is much like the unhealthy imprinting where parents, without conscious effort, pass on bad habits to their children. Interestingly, neither the parents nor the children of this political phenomenon are necessarily outright ideological fanatics, for the intensity of adherence to core principles is not valued as is the taboo that the family members do not cross over to *the other side*.

Such individuals may be armed with convenient axioms like: "My grandparents were members of the party, my parents were members of the party, and I am therefore continuing a long and proud family tradition." Such vacuous statements only ensure that bad political affiliations are passed down from generation to generation. This would be fine in a static world, but that is not the world we live in or ever have, for that matter. As noted in a previous chapter, parasitic leftists are always seeking a host, and established political parties offer multiple benefits, one of which is a great cover for subterfuge. Once the leftist parasite quietly latches on to the targeted political party, party life will never be the same. In turn, over time, party leadership will slide ever leftward, until one day the new leadership is not the same as the daddy's or grand pappy's party!

The Static

So what happens when one's political leadership drifts leftward? It is at a juncture such as this that a logical (rather than emotional), contextual appraisal should be done and one's position reassessed. But alas, there are anchors that impede change—relational circles that have run the test of time, traditions or customs in which one has engaged in that have become second nature, and so on. To leave such a world is not easy and may not even seem necessary, especially for someone who is happy, content, and comfortable. Change can be difficult, especially when the comfortable and the familiar appear more attractive than the unknown. Humanity has a history of avoiding change, even at great costs.

Why is this? Consider the simplistic reasoning of change avoidance: take the path of least resistance or "go along to get along." From this standpoint, change is feared because of potential repercussions. If it happens that one reaches conclusions contrary to perceived group thought, even with maturity and conscious thought taking a strong foothold, one may still be reluctant to come out and take a stand for fear of economic retaliation, loss of friendships, and the eventuality of, well, more change! Demoralized by self-imposed defeat, these types carry on minimally through life, or as Henry David Thoreau said: "Most men lead lives of quiet desperation and go to the grave with the song still in them."

The Codependents

There are those who support the left because of personal interests, regardless of their personal beliefs. Some lend public support to the left because an alliance with the left is good for business and or possibly guarantees them position, power, or income. Some are just everyday citizens, being neither radical nor intertwined with the leftist political machine, who simply want to live life without interference. Yet, it is the very fear of interference that keeps them from freely expressing what they believe. These are those who have fallen prey to political correctness; they privately disagree with the leftist ideology and at the same time publicly shy away from any confrontation. The following illustrates this phenomenon.

Travel is a wonderful teacher, and whenever I travel abroad I learn to appreciate my own country as much as I learn to appreciate the countries I visit. One summer, I found my way to Istanbul, Turkey, a city in the crossroads of history; a city of empires long gone; a city where the West is conjoined with the East. In fact, Istanbul sits partly on the European continent and partly on the Asian continent, separated by a narrow strait, called the Bosporus, which links the Black Sea to the Mediterranean Sea. The geographic location and features of Istanbul cannot be understated, for many an empire has desired to control this land. Walking around Istanbul gives one a constant reminder of ancient history, and in some strange way, yesteryear appears just as close as yesterday. It was within this crucible of civilization where I had an eye-opening experience.

One day as I was walking with a fellow traveler, just outside the famed Blue Mosque, I noticed out of the corner of my eye a Turkish man, somewhere in his twenties, curiously smiling and peering at us. He was wearing business slacks, a collared shirt (no tie), and a sport coat. Even though I was not looking directly at him, I could tell that his eyes were tracking us as we strolled by. Just as we were about to pass him by, he threw out a salutation and a question all at once, and in Spanish. I knew enough Spanish to get the gist of what he was attempting to say, and I replied in English. Without effort, he switched to speaking English, and an amicable conversation ensued. It turns out that this curious Turk was an Oriental rug store owner, and his only curiosity was in selling us an Oriental rug. Little did he or I know where our innocent chat would eventually lead that day.

After a few minutes of cordial exchange, he invited us over to his showroom (within walking distance), where he offered to show us all the rugs that we would like to see. Even though we made it politely clear that we were not interested in a rug, being the consummate salesman, he did not easily give up. As we entered the showroom, he ordered (in Turkish) his assistant to bring us Turkish coffee and baklava. We declined graciously as the tray was put in front of us. "Are you sure?" he said, seeming somewhat baffled as to why we did not accept his offering. Nevertheless, he promptly returned to the main event: selling an Oriental rug. As he led us around the showroom, he would order his assistant to pull one rug and then another. Although it took a while, he eventually relinquished the notion that we were ever going to buy a rug.

By this time, however, fueled by our questions concerning the Turkish way of life and buoyed by his willingness to answer, the conversation about Oriental rugs had transformed into a discussion about Turkish culture. After realizing that a sale had escaped him, rather than thanking us and moving on to the next mark, he let his game face slip off and appeared to relax into his natural state. In an autonomic fashion, he pulled out a cigarette (he again offered, we again declined), lit up, and ordered his assistant to bring out something else. This time it was an array of liquor, which he offered to us, and again, we politely declined (I imagined him thinking to himself, *Do these people accept anything?*). Unperturbed, he grabbed his own glass and poured himself a drink. As our cross-cultural discussion continued, our newfound friend unconsciously demonstrated that he could carry on a conversation, balance a cigarette in his mouth, juggle a drink in his hands, and gesture with his arms in a symphonic manner. He was a *bon vivant* if I ever saw one, and a happy one at that.

The post-sales conversation was quite enjoyable, as could be expected, since Turkish people are renowned for their hospitality (for many of the individuals I met in Turkey, it was as if I had known them for a long time). We discussed a variety of topics: Turkish food, Turkish customs, and Turkish history. There was one area, however, of his culture in which he was unsure: religion. Whenever the conversation turned to the subject of Islam, he did not have many answers, and without any apparent shame, readily admitted his lack of knowledge.

As the time came for us to be moving on, we thanked our Turkish friend for his hospitality. As if desperate for something to offer us that would be accepted, he said if I could come back later that night, he would introduce me to some individuals at the nearby mosque who could answer our questions about Islam. He also made it clear that my fellow traveler, who was female, would not be able to attend. As we were with a group and she was interested in other aspects of Turkey, I accepted. Finally, something he had offered to which the answer was yes!

As planned, I later returned that evening to my newfound friend's rug shop. After some more "intercultural" exchange, he brought me over to the nearby mosque. We met in a small room with three men dressed in what I understood to be traditional Muslim garb. They did not speak English, at least not to me, so my "pro bono Turkish guide" provided the translation for both sides. We all talked cordially for quite some time—that is, until the conversation turned to alcohol. One of the Islamists stated that unlike in America, Muslims do not drink alcohol. I casually pointed toward my Turkish host and said innocently in English, "He drinks. Does that not make him a Mus[lim] …" I was abruptly cut off by the words, "Shut up," quietly but firmly and surprisingly, coming from my Turkish friend. It was at that moment that my happy-go-lucky, libertine host's demeanor completely changed. A new personality had arisen incongruous to the one I had witnessed previously. He then turned to the Islamists and rattled off something in Turkish. I immediately became sidelined as the discussion went back and forth between the Islamists and my Turkish friend. I sensed that I had overstepped some boundary and in deference to my friend, did my best to navigate an exit to the discussion. From that point on, my Turkish friend's demeanor was starkly different.

Upon convening our talk, I thanked the Islamists and followed my Turkish host as he strode out. Although doing his best to suppress his unease, he was visibly upset and would not say a word or look at me. As soon as we were far from earshot of the mosque (I realized later why he did this), he stopped, looked at me, and nervously pulled out a cigarette. He had a look like a master would look at his puppy who just did something wrong; the master, in frustration, trying to explain to the puppy the wrong the puppy did, is unable to punish the puppy because of the puppy's ignorance.

He recomposed himself and explained that, at that time in Turkey, the Islamists that we were talking to were not of any consequence. However, should the day come when their kind of Muslims come into political power, they would push for religious law to become the law of the land. Consequently, they would come after people like him: non-practicing Muslims. It was striking to see the fear in his eyes and the change in body language from just a few hours ago when he was a free-wheeling entrepreneur. Amazingly, the fear of potential retribution in the future was enough for him to watch what he said and did in the present.

Perhaps being a native of Istanbul gave him a constant reminder of history and in some strange way, that yesteryear was just as close as yesterday and, more importantly, that yesteryear could repeat itself at any time in the future. In the final analysis, my libertine friend had already been beaten by the Islamists, for they had convinced him to suppress his views. They had already convinced him to fear the future with all of its possibilities—not to mention making him fear the present with all of its realities.

The Opportunists

These are the natural-born bloodsuckers of society—you know them, you may even be related to one or more of them: self-centered individuals who care for nothing outside of their own skin. These are the types who would sell their mother's soul, their country's soul, or any soul, for that matter, for personal gain. These leftist henchmen are known for their talents that they have cultivated in leftist circles, and so they continue to practice in the area in which they are experienced and comfortable.

These types are pure political mercenaries, who would switch back and forth along the political spectrum if possible. But that would be, of course, detrimental to business. Subsequently, they are forced to take up one side for life. Such types are pure opportunists. They care nothing for the left or the right; they only care for themselves, but because they abet the left, they are a bona fide menace to society.

The Servile

There are those followers whose allegiance fills an emotional void. Lefty recognizes them for who they are and manipulates them for full advantage. They can be so psychologically twisted that, in a strange way, they seem to feed off of leftist approval. The extremes of this type appear to have a boot-licking complex which, like the psychoses of their leftist masters, may be tied to a psychosis developed during their early years. They are easily recognized by their duplicitous nature. On one hand, they will relentlessly spew venomous hate at those on the political right for their unwillingness to bend to their psychotic demands. Yet at the same time, they will treat tyrannical regimes with kid gloves, even lavishing praise on them and treating them as royalty. Even with their defective set of neurons, they understand all too well that those on the right will not persecute them like those on the left would.

Picture a Chihuahua in a defiant stance in front of a tank, barking at the casual passerby. Imagine the tank represents the constitution of a republic, the Chihuahua represents the liberal, and the passerby represents the conservative. The constitution of the republic, like a tank, is a device that conservatives respect and revere, knowing that its strength is the source of their liberties. Liberals, on the other hand, abhor the constitution and look forward to replacing it with their own ideological code. Until that day arrives, however, liberals will use the constitution to their advantage. Thus, with the constitution behind them, liberals travail through all kinds of machinations and contortions, lashing out against conservatives. Quite smugly, they know that the idea of harming someone because of political beliefs, no matter how bad, is neither part of the constitution nor part of the conservatives' DNA.

On the other hand, liberals are also the purest of cowards, not knowing how to say no to anyone unless they are sure that person will not harm them. When they sense that someone can and will hurt them for speaking out (without a constitution to back them up), they curiously remain silent and surprisingly become very cordial. In the liberal mindset, brutal tyrants who threaten other nations, murder their own citizens, and generally cause problems for the rest of the globe are somehow worthy of a friendly diplomatic mission. This leaves one with only a few conclusions about these special leftists, and that is they:

1. Admire the brutal tyrants and see them as role models.

2. Consider brutal tyrants to be allies in the war on freedom.

3. Sense that at some time in the future a brutal tyrant may have the opportunity or the power to modify their existence (so be nice!).

4. See these brutal tyrants as their dark lord and master who they have dreamed of serving all of their life.

This may explain why liberals embrace criminal elements, dictators, and the like: such individuals may at some point either spare their life or prove to be nefariously useful. And this, above all, shows why liberals are truly cowards and should not be anywhere near the seats of power and influence. Liberals in high places have and will sacrifice all that is necessary for their own preservation and selfish needs. Correspondingly, they will have no concern about the consequences to the rest of society.

How often have we seen certain left-leaning politicians or entertainers disparage an elected conservative? These leftists reside in a free constitutional republic and know that the right-leaning individuals they rail against will not harm them, so they attack. At the same time, there are countries where these cowards would not even dare say an unkind whisper in secret concerning the leadership. In those countries, they know that for the slightest infraction they could be shuffled off to the nearest stadium, alas, not for the purpose of a rallying speech or an inspiring performance, but to be executed!

25

The Myopic Ideologues

The one-issue ideologues: the secularists (the anti-religious crowd), the gun haters (the anti-self protection crowd), the abortionists (the anti-other protection crowd), etc. These are groups and individuals who, by pushing their cause, willingly or unwillingly enable Lefty to fulfill the ultimate goal of power and control. They live in a realm devoid of common sense and for that matter do not want to see or hear contradicting information. They are the rabid of the rabid.

Take the right to self-defense: if a loved one is killed by a criminal that happens to use a gun, it is understandable why one's gut reaction may be against firearms. A weapon-free world would be a dream, but that is all it is. As long as man breathes, there will be those who willfully use violence against others, whether it is with guns or other means.

Because criminals will always get their hands on weapons, citizens need to be able to combat that power; they need equal access. Gun laws only serve to take away the power from law-abiding citizens. Criminals by their very definition do not obey the law, and subsequently, there are many laws that do not affect the commission of a crime, period. If you think making firearms illegal will take them off the streets, look at what it has done for illegal drugs. Criminal and leftist elements in foreign countries line up to sell drugs to other countries. They same scenario would happen with firearms—and only criminals would have them. Myopic ideologues want to hear nothing from the opposite side, for they only want to have it their way. Like leftists, they only want a one-sided conversation.

The Ideologues

These are the most dangerous of all followers. They actually believe that the answer is in the Kool-Aid they are given to drink. They exist in varying degrees of intensity and allegiance; the most indoctrinated will blindly carry out the dictates of a maniac in chief. Not that such types do not become disillusioned with time and maturity, but in the primal stages they can do nothing but live, eat, and breathe the leftist dogma.

They are not necessarily deranged individuals. In fact, they can be quite decent individuals of high faith. They have to be—they believe in the leftist cause and that its ultimate goal will be of benefit to all mankind. Unlike the other groups, these adherents generally come from a certain segment of society: they tend to be young, optimistic, hopeful, and most importantly, gullible. *Their outlook on life and the world is heavily influenced by the youthful stage of life they find themselves in—unwise in the ways of the world while at the same time having seen enough of its disparity.* Thus, they desire to see real change and predictably latch on to the message of the latest leftist messiah.

The Final Solution

There comes a time when the aggregation of all the leftist followers reaches a critical mass and all factions begin to march in sync. When this happens, the puppet master giddily leads the gaggle of groups in a grand parade to the throne of power. For some of the puppets, there is a belief that they are being led to a world of ecstatic harmony where all of their life's issues are resolved; for others, they do not know anything about the puppet master's ideas or direction but simply want to be part of the parade; while others, lacking the strength and courage to resist, march mechanically toward the awaiting abyss. All the while, unbeknownst to most, the pied puppet master only has one goal in mind: consolidation of power.

Should the puppet master reach the goal, the parade leads to the destruction of the framework of society. Here, in a nutshell, is the basic outline of the leftist trek: promising a better future than what the present has to offer while leading society to a state that is worse than it was before.

Not all is lost, however, for beyond the outskirts of the parade stands a group not yet accounted for: those who see the puppet master for who he or she is. These are the ones who do not follow in lock step and never will. They are the patriotic, the conservative, the humble, the free, and the independent thinkers who cherish life and liberty. It is only from within this vein of independence where deliverance from the leftist death march is possible.

Words

> *"Thanks to words, we have been able to rise*
> *above the brutes; and thanks to words, we*
> *have often sunk to the level of demons."*
>
> **—Aldous Huxley**

Words, each unto themselves, may seem insignificant. Nothing more than definitions that can be plucked out of any dictionary, correct? Yet history has shown that mere words have the power to move millions, sweep them up in hypnotic fervor, and drive them to highs and lows they never imagined. Countries have been birthed by mere words on paper. The laws that govern our daily lives are nothing more than words on paper, yet countries would not exist or operate without those *mere* words. Words, when polished, are very powerful and have the ability to change minds, shape movements, and create nations; and as well, to destroy them.

Leftists understand and appreciate the power of words. Word manipulation is the primary tool used in the leftist arsenal of political weapons. They love words—that is, as long as they have a monopoly on them. Ironically, and yet understandably, they hate free speech. It is no mere coincidence that the first amendment of the U. S.

constitution, the first right in the Bill of Rights, is the right to free speech. It reads as follows:

> *"Congress shall make no law respecting an establishment of religion, or prohibiting the free exercise thereof; or abridging the freedom of speech, or of the press; or the right of the people peaceably to assemble, and to petition the government for a redress of grievances."*

Free speech is the foundational tenet of a free society and likewise the very freedom that leftist despots from time immemorial have abhorred. Why? Because it sews into the political fabric the right to use words to freely express grievances against the governing political body without fear of retaliation or oppression. From the leftist point of view, it allows for disagreement with, and consequently opposition to, leftist propaganda.

Is it not ironic that, for the left, the right to free speech is what they loathe the most, yet at the same time the very right they abuse above all other freedoms? Ironic as well is that the exploitation of this foundational freedom is used to gain traction for sinister agendas. And if that is not enough irony, the freedom of speech is the very vehicle by which the left is allowed, by a free society, to deliver propaganda *en masse*. But even with such a gift handed out on a silver platter, leftists who want to succeed must be disciplined in the manipulation of word and prose. Even with assistance from fellow sympathizers and useful idiots entrenched in the media, a natural prerequisite is that up and coming statists be well versed in communication exploitation.

The trick for any aspiring *dictocrat* is to craft a message so that the true desired outcome is not exposed. In other words, to offer humanity a greater place than they are in now while herding them into the leftist abyss without the herd ever realizing the end game. It is a story with a political slogan as old as time: "Give me your trust and I will deliver a better tomorrow!"

The basic setup is quite simple. Up front, the leftist presents himself as a "public servant." From where the masses stand, they most likely want to be better off than their present stead or at the very least the same, certainly not worse. In the initial political negotiation, this scenario may seem like a win-win. The leftist wants to be the "public servant," and the masses want to better their lot in life. The perception, however, is far from the horrific reality. The underlying truth is that the leftist wants to be in complete control and could care less if anyone's life ever improves, or only to the extent that it will further his or her goals. In fact, when the leftist dream is finally accomplished, very few will even have a position to improve.

The fact that we give such miscreants an audience is possibly deeply rooted in our psyche. Religious and cultural influences may play a role in germinating and reinforcing the notion. Creation stories abound around the world regarding man's descent from some deity, metaphysical being, or altered state. The basic thread that seems to prevail throughout these explanations of our not-so-humble beginnings is that we once had a better existence or were at least *more* connected to the celestial. Perhaps in our subconscious we sense that we have since fallen to a lower station and naturally long to reconnect to a heavenly existence.

Conversely, just as there are many creation stories, many cultures/religions have a final chapter. In a good number of these scenarios, a messiah type returns to either whisk away the believers to a paradise and/or restores the earth to a paradise. For Jews, it is the Messiah; for Christians, it is Jesus Christ; for Orthodox Sunni Muslims, it is Muntazar; for Shiite Muslims, it is the Twelfth Imam; for mainstream Buddhists, it is the Maitreya; for Hindus, it is Kalki or Javada; and the list goes on ...[7]

In a sense, such beliefs may assist Lefty in his plans. People may somehow feel that they are living in a misplaced existence and hence, are looking for the return of a savior, or a messianic figure to reconnect us to our glorious beginnings and initiate a glorious future. To this end, the left is more than happy to provide a substitute: a counterfeit. They are more than happy to dupe the world into entering into the leftist version of paradise. And it all

---

7   *http://www.mt.net/~watcher/namethatmessiah.html*

starts, as we will learn, with methods and tactics that manipulate the basic building blocks of language: words.

Substitution

Substitution is the method of substituting a word or phrase to disguise what one actually means. In the following examples, *original* denotes what the leftist truly means, while *substituted* denotes what the leftist actually says. For example:

Original: We simply want *superiority*.
Substituted: We simply want *equality*.

There are several subconscious aspects of the *second* statement that appeal to one's sense of fairness: 1) all they want is to be on the same level with everyone else. 2) By the very statement, they are indicating that they are at a disadvantage in their present situation. 3) Resolution is simple: let them have the same rights as anybody else. Nothing to lose there, correct? After all, there have been legitimate movements in history that have had equality as a legitimate goal.

But one finds another storyline when surveying the leftist political movements of the past. In some form or another, most of them basically pushed the message of equality for all. If they were truly being sincere in their aims, such a proposal would have merit. Never forget who we are talking about: leftists. The truth is that any agenda the left is advancing is never about equality and is always about superiority. Let's take a look at another one:

Original: We need more money for *indoctrination*.
Substituted: We need more money for *education*.

Again, there are several subconscious aspects to the second statement: 1) Education is a great thing, and who could argue against better education. After all, it is for the children! 2) Wrapped inside the very statement is an implied under-funding and hence an under-education. 3) The public can support this effort by demanding more education dollars.

Once again, it is not more education or child enrichment they seek but rather personal enrichment and reinforcement of a system that will assist them in taking over the education system. In turn, the goal is that indoctrination will increase and therefore pave the way for the triumphal rise to power. As usual, the children are nothing more than convenient pawns in the leftist Ponzi scheme. Programs that are marketed as "for the children" usually do more harm to the very children they espouse to want to help. Such is the way of leftist outcomes. Let's look at another example, with multiple substitutions and rephrasing:

Original: We need to *infiltrate* and *control* the culture.
Substituted: Society is better *served* by a *diverse* workforce.

Looking at the second statement, here come the mind tricks again: 1) Diversity allows for different points of view, allowing for s broader perspective. 2) The very statement implies that we are shutting out valuable individuals from the process, not only in disenfranchising them but taking value away from ourselves.

Here is the real meaning: Lefty wants to provide a path for unacceptable ideas to be granted acceptance in the mainstream and to prepare the cultural ground for when harvest time arrives. In other words, diversity promotion is the process of cultural ground tilling in preparation for firmly planting leftist ideas. Just as education dollars are not really for the children but for *educrats* and radical education agendas, diversity programs are not really for racial minorities but for race mongers and radical social agendas.

Amelioration

There are some words that are just negative no matter what context they are used in, so leftists must define them in improved or more neutral terms. One of the best examples is the word "terrorist." There is no amount of speech that can assist someone in trying to show support for a terrorist.

Take the phrase, "I support the terrorists because ..." After hearing the word "terrorists," the speaker has lost you. However, if the word "terrorist" is merely changed to "insurgent," as for example, "I support the insurgents because …" you may step back and listen. Your mind may pause and consider that this is a legitimate person speaking on behalf of a legitimate cause. Instead of your sympathies being shut down automatically by hearing the word "terrorists," the word "insurgents" may lead to a neutral or possibly positive response by changing a mere word!

There are a lot of similarities in leftist propaganda and sales. What amelioration does is bridge the banal to the benign wrapped in a political sales pitch. Always remember, the left is always trying to sell you on their loosely constructed vision. And selling, as has been reiterated countless times in sales seminars the world over, is an emotional event. The main focus of the outcome is about how you *feel* about the product, or in this case, the message. Rarely are disconcerting facts bandied about, for these would light up your logical nature and an undesired outcome may occur. Your logical nature may then begin to counteract your emotional one.

And of course, Lefty does not want logic to ever enter into the picture. The goal is to keep the emotional receptors front and center in your mind. This is very important to grasp: leftists primarily want to appeal to and manipulate your emotional nature, because with pure emotions, there are no facts and figures, science, or history (unless they are omitted, twisted, or revised) with which to contend, just an emotional appeal that impacts how we feel and hence, how we perceive.

Redefinition

There are words that evoke nothing but positive thoughts. There are words that you don't need to disguise and then there are words that evoke negative thoughts. And Lefty knows he must avoid them at all costs and, if possible, they must be eradicated. Redefinition makes use of the psychological principle known as association. The type of association for this discussion is similar to the notion that human beings link people, places, things, and events with emotions.

For example, we may associate hot cocoa with a fireplace because when we were young our mother would make us hot cocoa and we would sit by the fireplace. This is a positive association. On the contrary, we may have been bitten by a dog the first time we met one. From then on, we may associate dogs with being bitten (i.e. a painful memory). This is an example of a negative association.

When looking to rebrand a negative association, Lefty chooses a word with a history of positive association to then disguise his agenda. Take the word *choice*. In popular culture, decades ago, choice generally meant to have your pick of something, the end result typically being positive; one typically chose and received something positive. Today, the word choice has been redefined to mean *abortion*. In this twisted vernacular, the actual result of choice is negative. One party in the process receives a death sentence; the surviving party may be subject to an existence mired in guilt and possible long-term medical complications (like sterility, breast cancer, or even death). All is not bleak, however, for there is a positive outcome for one of the participants: the abortionist generates some cash flow.

"Choice" is a word that years ago had a unique context and meaning but also has been co-opted to the point that it can never be purely used in that context again. This is typical of what leftists of all stripes do: they steal customs, language, and history to justify their means and satisfy their wants, to the ruination of society.

Inversion

At this point, it should be evident that the definition of what the average person perceives and what the leftist actually means are usually two opposing ideas. The tactic of inversion wholly embodies this type of word manipulation. Inversion is the practice of using an antonym or a juxtaposed term of a word to describe and summarily whitewash the true meaning. By doing so, inversion sets up the receptors in your brain to accept the message rather than reject it. In the original delivery, the message is a threat. In an inverted (although twisted) delivery, the message has an appeal to our higher nature.

In the book *1984* (note, a fictional account), inversion is the government's attempt to whitewash its activities. Love was torture:

the Ministry of Love was actually a torture chamber; education was indoctrination: the Ministry of Education was actually a brainwashing outfit; war was peace: the Ministry of Peace was constantly waging war. The big brother government of 1984 used juxtaposed terms to present a cleansed marquee, disguising the real activity of the organization.

The switch is not always negative to positive, however. In today's vernacular, the term "hate" has been used to describe activity that is contrary to the leftist ideology. For example, *hate speech* is anything that speaks in opposition to leftist dogma. Traditionally, we know hate speech as free speech—by using "hate" in place of "free," the left has inverted the term to fit into their emotional confines.

Even more egregious than *hate speech* is *hate crimes*. These are crimes that are classified not only by your actions, but your thoughts as well. Under hate crime legislation, both your actions and your thoughts are subject to prosecution. This is the kind of persecution that really gets the left excited—one can picture them muttering in a Gollum-like fashion: *"We, my precious (add some salivating and some snickering), can even go after your thoughts, so be careful what you think!"*

The slippery logic gets worse. Follow this frightening example of leftist reasoning:

> *If a person had hateful thoughts and then acted upon them, one could conclude that preventing their hateful thoughts may have prevented the hateful act. Therefore, those hateful thoughts must be stopped before they can be acted upon. Not only is there an obvious need for laws deterring hate crime, there is also a need for laws deterring hate speech. Such hateful speech must be squelched and coupled with punitive measures enacted to bolster deterrence.*
>
> *After all, we cannot let these monsters spread their vicious hate. As an additional measure, to further ensure that such hate does not infect our society, such rogue individuals must subject themselves to rehabilitation (translation: re-education camps) and our children should be inoculated via education (translation: pre-education camps), exposing the dangers of such discourse. After all, it is for the protection of us all.*

Sound reasonable? First, all violent crimes have some element of hate. Second, crimes that are typically designated as "hate crimes" are meant to silent opposition to an agenda. Third, "hate" crimes are charged based on the victim's social status, not the crime itself. This means that any two criminals will be prosecuted differently for the same crime, and that some victims will receive more "justice" than others, for the same crime! In summary, the only hate going on in the example above is the hate the left has for freedom of speech and freedom of thought ... oh, and life, liberty, and the pursuit of happiness.

Labeling

Labeling is used to paint the opposition with the negative. The ultimate aim is to portray the opposition (usually anyone on the political right) in as negative of a light as possible, while painting those on the left in as positive of a light as possible. Negative terms are used to describe the opposition and their actions, while positive terms are used to portray leftist agents and their actions. One of the best examples to examine is that old leftist favorite, death.

Groups on the political right are conveniently prefixed with the "anti" label. When combined with another negative term, even though giving it a positive outcome, it sounds even worse. Take the term "anti-abortion," which really means "against infanticide" or "for life." But one must admit that it sounds like a type of person who is negative and focused on a negative issue. That's not someone you generally want to be around (note again the recurring theme of the power of words evoking feelings). On the other hand, the term "pro-choice" sounds better, possibly because it is two positive sounding words. Yet today, the term translates to "in favor of infanticide" or "for death"!

If you are one of those who is fully informed on the issues, this subject may not have such a penetrating effect on your psyche. As well, a mature person may not see the significance of this, but one should not underestimate the subliminal impact on a mature adult. But even more critical is the impact it can have on the young and the uninformed—the primary target audience of the left. Imagine if you were new to the whole concept of abortion and were given a biased presentation sprinkled with these terms. Which way would you naturally sway?

It may appear that with all the word manipulation techniques discussed so far, one technique may seem technically very similar to another. As such, this small study in word manipulation may not bear significance to some, but to the leftist it is of extreme importance, because beyond the "how," it is the "why" that is much more important to comprehend. And the "why" can best be summed up as follows:

1. Words have meaning.
2. Meaning influences perception.
3. Perception influences outcome.
4. Outcome determines control.
5. Control is power.

Words have power.

Word power is real. Next time you watch, listen to, or read the news, isolate the words used as opposed to the storyline. In essence, parse the wording. You may discern that there is a whole lot of word manipulation happening to influence how you perceive the subject of the story. You may be amazed by what you have been missing all these years.

Message

"The magic of the tongue is the most dangerous of all spells."
—Edward Bulwer-Lytton

Understanding how to manipulate words is one thing; entering into actual discourse is another. Any fool can belt out a pearl-handled phrase once in a while, but to consistently chain words together and paint a picture in the mind's eye is an art, an art in which successful leftists are well versed. Lefty instinctively knows that message mastery is king and will, when well executed, efficiently draw in prey.

A strong argument can be made that the left spends more time focused on message crafting than on substance and analysis combined. This may explain why, in the end, the only real deliverable message the left has is a hopeful-sounding one. Any true analysis reveals Lefty's *scheme du jour* for what it is—pure vaporware. To be fair, however, there may be some aspects of truth in any given leftist message, but that is akin to saying a loaf of moldy bread still has some decent corners on it.

In any event, substance does not matter since leftists are not interested in ever delivering on it. And since they only desire one outcome, as in, *they rule and we submit,* the process is better facilitated by having a one-way conversation, as in, *they speak and we listen.* To the leftist, an interactive conversation which happens in a free society is disdained and to be avoided. Disappointingly for the left, an inquiry-free ascendancy to power is practically impossible within the framework of a vibrant, free society. And so, reluctantly, the leftist message artist must step into the stream of political discourse, knowing it is the only way to seed dangerous ideas, draw in converts, and infiltrate the seats of influence and power.

Even so, open debate is feared and to be avoided whenever possible, for it has the potential to expose unattractive facets at any given point, for open dialogue is exposure, and exposure to the light of truth is fatalistic. If it were possible, Lefty would declare any form of debate to be against the law. Yet even Lefty realizes that the extinction of free public discourse will have to wait until he and his comrades realize the dream of *dictatorus maximus.*

It should be noted, however, that refusing a debate is not necessarily the same as avoiding a debate. That is, a legitimate individual would not be hiding something if choosing to opt out of a debate. Sometimes it is prudent not to lower oneself or give audience or credence to an individual who is bordering on insanity.

With that said, let's explore the various techniques that Lefty uses to redirect, discourage, and generate debate for the purpose of influencing the *target* audience, highlight the word *target*. Note that the term *debate*, for the purpose of this discussion, is used in the general sense, as an umbrella term covering a multitude of scenarios: as being defined as a formal debate between two human beings; an ongoing public discussion in the media; a national debate that is comprised of points and counterpoints made by articles, talking heads, and the like. Such debates can go on and on for decades.

Minimization

Minimization is the notion that any negative outcome reflecting on the leftist agenda needs to be minimized. Interestingly, this would also include any *positive* outcome for the political right since such an occurrence is the equivalent of a negative outcome for the left! Minimization is accomplished by a variety of techniques:

explaining away the actions, ignoring primary motives, redirecting the conversation to any tangent available, etc.

Take the issue of abstinence education. While study after study will show that it is effective, leftist mouthpieces will explain it away with catch words like "simplistic," "unrealistic," or "outdated." In effect, they *minimize* the importance of the statistical information. Yet, when confronted with the tsunami of communicable diseases and adolescent pregnancies, the left will never mention that these outcomes are a result of leftist policy and propaganda. Again, they will *minimize* the importance of the statistical information. Instead, they might lament on the unfortunate state of affairs, explaining how the root of the problem is "complex," and possibly summarily redirect the conversation to the "obvious need for more comprehensive education."

The underlying reality is that the sole purpose of any leftist policy is to further an agenda. They know that what they are doing might be offensive or damaging, but that does not matter to them; it is part of the plan. Leftist policies are designed to be as subtle as possible by pushing the envelope, landing just shy of ripping it wide open. The only mystery in the mix, to Lefty, is the potential level of public reaction. No worries for Lefty, however, for he has a contingency plan: minimization.

One must understand that you and yours are constantly being sold and marketed an agenda, piece by piece, until you are steeped in the mire so deep that there is no escape. The whole purpose of minimizing is to inform you that such infractions are not really as bad as they seem and that they are not going to destroy your world. Agenda drivers use minimization to leave you feeling that everything is really fine and there is no need to worry. It is as if they are saying, "Don't worry, your country, your culture, and your values will be there in the morning when you get up. Now go back to sleep!"

Maximization

The opposite of minimization is maximization or the "many out of none" proposition. Whenever the left has success, the perception of success, or even feigned success, the exposure of that outcome is maximized as much as possible. In maximization, the premise is born from a notion, theory, or an outright lie that are expounded and expanded upon over and over. Over time, the original idea itself becomes anathema, for how it furthers the leftist agenda is of prime importance.

Maximization could also be defined as the constant drone of propaganda being released, modified, and re-released again: the old saying that if you tell a lie enough times it will become accepted as fact rings true in this sense. Leftists love to throw out ideas that cannot be easily proved, yet have some grain of plausibility. Take the theory of evolution: one cannot prove it, yet the message is constantly regenerated and repackaged time and time again until it is casually bandied about as fact.

As well as building a "rep" for the idea, maximization provides Lefty some additional benefits. First, it can keep the public arguing about the merits of an issue while deflecting attention away from other stealth activities. What do you think the left would rather discuss: their plan to run a country into the ground and summarily take over or environmental issues? Second, by pushing the envelope, so to speak, Lefty keeps the opposition busy on defense while formulating plans for the next offensive foray. Such straw man agendas can be quite useful by diverting attention from real issues. Third, but just as important as the other two, it can birth the "need" to enact legislation, of which the prime purpose is to further leftist encroachment.

The distribution of the maximized propaganda is handled through a variety of sympathetic drones in various outlets: the media, government, and public and private institutions. As you may have already concluded, maximization is generally an offensive tactic, whereas minimization is generally a defensive one. Yet these seemingly polar opposites both have one tactic in common: silencing.

Silencing

A dream of leftists is to have their agendas roll through society without opposition: to infiltrate the culture with a maximum amount of saturation without awakening the citizenry and if it were possible, without saying a word. Such a feat can be accomplished in part by the technique of silencing. Silencing is the tactic of squashing partially or entirely any discussion on an issue.

For example, say a *leftist* judge is discovered to be engaged in illegal activity. The story may quietly appear in the "B" section of the newspaper, in a small, hardly noticeable blurb. After the story is printed once, it is dropped, never to be raised again (as a tangential benefit, the entire press now has an alibi that the matter has been reported). This is an example of silencing in a defensive manner.

On the other hand, if a judge is a conservative and commits an innocent, albeit legal, procedural error, his name will make the front page for weeks! His name and actions will be magnified and constantly flashed in a negative silhouette in all the leftist media organs until he is hounded from the bench. In this sense, the message is *maximized* for exposure—no silencing here!

Later on, if the question of disparate treatment by the media of the two judges arises, the media turns to the tactic of *minimization*. They will argue that the story of the leftist judge was not that important of a story, or at the time (conveniently), there were other pressing stories that warranted attention—basically any excuse to wiggle out of the truth. Unfortunately, by time this happens, the time for society to react has passed and the left has already moved on to the next offensive move.

Silencing is a favorite tool to squash debate on a whole list of issues, where only one side of the story is *maximized*, effectively disallowing an opposing view to surface. In this scenario, society is relentlessly subjected to a serial one-sided debate on the subject, scarcely hearing an opposing viewpoint. The public is never made aware of this slighting; it is only fed a unilateral argument wrapped up in leftist pretentiousness. Some relevant examples in this genre would include debates about firearms, abortion, and evolution.

For example, with firearms we are constantly told how many lives are lost, but we are never told how many lives are saved—never about how many crimes are prevented. Likewise, with abortion we are told of the rights to one's own body but never about the potential side effects; we are never told about the potential for death, infection, and infertility that may occur as the result of abortion, never told about the guilt, depressions, and lifelong emotional effects, never informed of maladies that can happen to that same body of which we hold those rights so dearly. As well, with the **theory** *of evolution* we are told that we evolved but never exactly how; never told that true transitional forms are nonexistent in the millions of examples in the fossil record; never told of all the discoveries that turned out to be not-so-human; never told about the many missing links in the neatly packaged story of evolution.

Equalization

When Lefty and/or one of his minions is caught red handed and has no way out of the situation, what does he do? He forcibly invites others to the party in the virtual, public paddy wagon. When caught with their hands in the public cookie jar or with the "cookies" themselves, leftists love to point out others who have gone down in similar disgrace and love to recount: "See! They did it too!" Consequently, when the one-man perp-walk swells to a parade of reluctant fingered sinners, Lefty fades into the parade, whispering, "See, I am not so bad after all. There are a lot of others you trusted who have done it too!" The whole purpose is, of course, to take the focus away from Lefty and his newly discovered transgression and to table any conversation on the topic.

The scheme starts out like this: once Lefty and company are exposed, the first order of the day is to find someone, living or dead, who has committed the same sin. The ruse works better if they are dead, so that they cannot defend or differentiate themselves. The dead-men-walking technique also allows Lefty to use his favorite tool: fabrication. It is quite a useful tool when dealing with the terminally unresponsive, because it allows Lefty to refinish his portrait with any palette of colors he desires.

However, if no candidate is available for exhumation, Lefty will attempt to harvest a live victim from the political right, initially leaving his party comrades alone. But if there are slim pickings on the right, the natural narcissism of a leftist drives him to pick one of his own. Such is the neurotic life of a leftist: the hunter and the hunted, of and by his own species.

Finally, once the hunted game is tagged, the hope is that the stigma, once only associated with the original leftist trespasser, is distributed among others, and therefore diminished, making Lefty look like not such a bad character after all. No matter the outcome, a tangential benefit of such a tagging is that it serves to degrade the image capital of the unwilling participant, dead or alive. It's even better if the target turns out to be an icon of the right, as far as Lefty is concerned.

In the end, leftists want the populace to believe that all are the same along the spectrum from the left to the right. The left wants to stretch the argument with the claim that if two individuals have the same personal peccadilloes, then they must be ideologically and philosophically on the same plane. Yet, humanity is too diverse and imperfect for such a claim. Political philosophy and personal actions do not always line up. Not only does Lefty want the rest of us to believe that there is no difference between the left and right, but to believe that, ultimately, we are all just like, well, Lefty! Lefty wants society to arrive at the conclusion that leftist ideas are just as acceptable as those on the right.

Not so fast. Take the issue of lying, which admittedly happens on the left and on the right. Lying, a leftist core value, is generally employed more often by those on the left than it is by those on the right. And just because it happens on the right does not make the right just like the left, and vice versa. Yet, without flinching, the left likes to claim equivalence by using the fact that there are *some* occurrences of lying on the right just like there are *many* occurrences of lying on the left. The left likes to claim equivalence.

However, that is the same as saying if a crime happens in a safe neighborhood, then that safe neighborhood is the equivalent of an unsafe neighborhood, where crimes happen more often. The correct statement is: crime generally occurs more in the unsafe neighborhood and crime generally occurs less in the safe neighborhood. Therefore, the conclusion is that one is generally more secure in the safe neighborhood than in the unsafe neighborhood. Using the illogic of the left, both are equally unsafe!

Adoption

This is the tactic of adopting an idea or general sentiment, even though the idea or sentiment itself is contrary to the leftist plans and core beliefs. In this case, leftists will publicly adopt an idea to increase their popularity, yet quietly detest the underlying principle of the idea. In essence, the leftist lends lip service to the general idea, while passive-aggressively keeping his true thoughts under wraps. Then, once enabled with power, Lefty uses the adopted issue to take the country in a different direction, usually a downward tailspin.

The latest of these examples is the question of a country's direction (as in moral, fiscal, etc.). For example, when polls show that the citizens are worried about the direction a country is headed, liberals jump on the bandwagon and heartily agree with public sentiment. On cue, liberals publicly feign the same general concern and express a desire to help. Naturally, citizens feel that someone is listening to them. The citizens are drawn toward this style of leadership, while all along, the left has another scheme in mind. With passion, liberals declare that if the public votes them in, they will fight to put the country in the "correct" direction (note: They typically say "right," but the irony would be just too much, besides being grammatically incorrect). What they leave out of their campaign rhetoric is exactly *what they define the correct direction to be*. Sure, to pacify the public, they will throw out some of the same empty promises as before. The sad irony is that after the public has been duped into voting for them, the masters of sophistry will continue to run the country aground and move it further in the wrong (left!) direction.

Switching

Switching means as one would switch a position on an issue. This is not a problem for a leftist, with or without allies in the media. Leftists, the best creative liars on the planet, are known to express conflicting beliefs, depending upon who they are addressing. Because the lie is an established institutional entity in the leftist realm, saying whatever one has to say to sway the crowd is perfectly acceptable. If by switching positions means going against one's personal beliefs, no problem; if it means throwing overboard a political ally, no problem. Self-preservation and empowerment are of supreme priority.

Make no mistake, being a leftist is not an easy road. One must have the instincts and qualities of a liar, a traitor, a deceiver, a narcissistic self-loather, and a consummate tyrant. And in the process of empowerment, one becomes paranoid and ultimately insane. The process of leftist empowerment not only destroys the target society, it can also psychologically degenerate the leftists themselves.

This may explain why switching comes so easy for such ilk. It is possibly a natural outcome of the psychological degeneration that naturally occurs in leftist devolution. Correspondingly, the condition appears to become more noticeable as the years go on: leftists are not bothered by glaring contradictions in their story, only surprised when someone points them out. It appears that this transfiguration is akin to the Dr. Jekyll syndrome: having to imbibe ever-increasing doses of the potion, Dr. Jekyll becomes the heinous Mr. Hyde permanently, having lost the ability to ever revert to his former self.

Groupies Think

Leftists love to create and throw around studies, experts, and commissions to give credence to their agenda, even tout data favorable to a cause backed by a pseudo-study or a faux committee. One will read and hear the following phrases, "experts say" or "the (fill in the blank) commission reported" or "studies on (fill in the blank) have shown" or "or more proponents/opponents say" or "reliable sources say." These statements beg the question: who deemed "them" reliable, trustworthy, accurate, or unbiased? Who did these studies? Who made these statements? All such types of faux-endorsed statements are short quips, planted in the hopes that the listener will quickly pass over them en route to the main information.

For such missives, details are not supposed to be known or asked. Remember, Lefty does not want an open discussion. If one dives into the details, the logic falls apart very quickly. To further persuade someone from inquiring, the dissuasive reasoning may sound something like the following:

> *The (fill in the blank) commission study on saving the children and the environment has concluded that our focus should be directed to the crisis at hand that if not solved, will endanger our very future! And all the opposition wants to focus on is insignificant details (translation: the origin of this information) that pale in comparison to the crisis (translation: the real insignificant detail!). Isn't it enough to know that we have a problem now? Is their head in the sand? Haven't the issues been discussed enough? It is time for action!*

If you still refuse to withdraw your questions, Lefty becomes more creative in obfuscation. Here is the crazy part: even when the sources are found to be frauds (the original premise for the "crisis"), leftists will still insist that it doesn't negate the fact that we still have a crisis that needs to be solved!

Numbers Game

Whenever possible, leftists always want to appear that they, and their issues, are on the side with the greater numbers. Leftists curiously assume and give the impression that the vast majority of the public believes in whatever the left is promoting. This is done so that anyone who does not fully believe the propaganda is purposely made to feel isolated or out of touch. Even though the proposition may be an outright lie, making one question one's own ideas is the intent. The implied question is: "Who are you to question and stand up against such a human tide of opinion?"

The numbers game is where one or two insignificant studies are the equivalent of "many" significant studies; where one or two pseudo-experts are the equivalent of "many" experts; where radical groups declare boldly (more like bold-faced), that they represent the majority of the public. And oh, by the way, what about those who don't agree with the leftist dogma? They are labeled, as you might have guessed, in the minority! The fact is that leftist groups typically represent a radicalized and highly organized vocal few who have a monopoly on free time and "sugar daddy" money. So while the majority of people are busy raising their families and making a living, subsidized radical socialists are bombarding the public airwaves with their propaganda.

Euphemizing

The socialist paradise is a land built upon euphemisms. When Lefty throws out euphemisms, he proposes something so wonderful and beautiful that one cannot imagine rejecting it. For example, soak up the following typical dreamy blather:

> *I long for the day when all people can visit a doctor without worry. Free from the confines of our present situation, all will be cared for, young and old alike. I believe only then will we truly have a productive and healthy society, which is why we must understand that universal healthcare is the ultimate issue of our time, above all others. When this right is secured, our country will be on the path to fulfill its great promise and reach its great potential.*

Sounds beautiful, doesn't it? It is dreamy and powerful in all its allegory, is it not? Its goal is to impress upon the listener that there exists a much higher plane that we can all reach together, in this case, if only medicine can be socialized! Even if there is no direct benefit to the listener, this message is designed to appeal to one's philanthropic nature.

Of course, the purpose of putting a euphemistic skin on a message is to convince the populace that mankind can solve our problems within the confines of a man-made paradise. Euphemisms offer a mental escape from the plane of reality where an individual's imagination can extrapolate to the stars. Once in a euphemistic trance, one can actually start to feel good about his or her prospects, where hope was ere absent. It is important to remember here that feeling, not substance, is the key deliverable for leftists. The euphemistic message can be summed up as this: "Trust me to take you on this journey, and your dreams will be realized!" Needless to say, history has another story to tell when it comes to the promised man-made paradises of yesteryear.

Balancing

Balancing is a favorite tool of the left that allows them to have their cake and eat it too. Balancing is a convenient vehicle to allay concerns and fears on both sides of an issue. Here is a typical example:

> *I believe in common sense gun laws and likewise understand the need for citizens' rights to be protected.*

You can be sure of one thing, the fascist falls sharply, and radically, on one side of the issue. The same words uttered by a true patriotic leader would be fine, but then again, there is a huge difference between a patriot and a fascist. Fascists are nothing more than political counterfeits portraying themselves as the real McCoy. It is of prime importance to know who the speaker is first, and then their words can be weighed. The old admonition, "Show me your friends and I will show you who you are" can be a fairly accurate measuring stick in these matters.

When enlisting balancing, the perpetrator does his or her best to avoid specifics. The leftist wants the issue to remain in the stratosphere, far from inspection. Details will trip them up and ultimately unmask who they really are, not what they pretend to be. In light of this last statement, the above example, emanating from a fascist, could best be translated as:

> *Common sense—that which the leftist deems appropriate.*
> *Citizens' rights—those few rights the leftist deems appropriate.*

With the resulting rewrite:

> *I believe in common sense laws that I deem appropriate and the few citizen rights that I deem appropriate to be protected.*

Balancing can be tricky, however. Once a balanced statement is made by a garden variety socialist, future events will raise questions:

"Where do you stand on (fill in the blank), based on your previous statement?" But alas, no worry for Lefty, for as we have already seen, the leftist has an array of tactics to revert to, should the situation present itself.

Imagery

Images act as silent megaphones, void of speech, yet yielding an effect much more powerful than countless words. Images have the power to transform a tyrannical dictator to a benevolent father figure, or a radical leftist into "just one of the folk." The left uses imagery to attract converts and simultaneously soften the edges of a public figure. In contrast, this visual tactic is used to destroy the image of the opposition (that would be the political right or anyone who believes in life, liberty, and the pursuit of happiness).

Leftist manipulation of imagery can be a multidimensional experience, where staging can be just as important. For example, socialists will place traditional, national symbols behind them or will be seen with elder statesmen, in whom the people have an established trust (note the manipulative use of the principle of association)—all done to show the public that they are just as true blue patriotic as anyone else.

Once his message is crafted and delivered, Lefty is ready for action, ready to grab the reigns of power and fight for control. Throughout the process of this oratorical phalanx, the public mind is constantly being "opened"—leftist code for seeding doubt about the tried and true, and the pouring in of the failed and false. Of course, leftist dogma is always marketed as new, but there is nothing new about it. The only new aspect to leftist propaganda is the calendar date and clothing styles.

In all the left says and does, they are preparing the culture for what they want to do when power is laid in their hands. Just as with parsing words, if one listens closely to the fabricated message, one can hear what they are really saying. Just like the sirens of Ulysses, the left appears beautiful and inviting, hypnotically drawing the culture closer and closer, until it dashes against the rocks.

Prelude

"Those who vote decide nothing. Those who count the vote decide everything."

—Joseph Stalin

As duly noted, Lefty does not like to enter into an open debate and participate in the free exchange of ideas. Rather, he prefers to have a one-sided conversation, accompanied by little or no opposition. However, while still operating and living in a free society, Lefty must put up with freedom's prerequisites until he gets a stranglehold. Until that time, Lefty employs a plethora of tactics to defeat, divert, and stave off the opposition. Notice what is being said here: to defeat, divert, or stave off the *opposition,* as opposed to defeating the *ideas* of the opposition.

Such tactics are a must, because in a true debate on substance, Lefty will invariably lose. Therefore, Lefty must constantly redirect the conversation away from substance and on to the imperfections of the opponents themselves. In line with this doctrine, the hypocritical nature of the left means that leftists are rarely guilty of any wrongdoing, nor should they ever be accused of any negative behavior. This leftist view of the world is colored with a self-comforting double standard: the opposition's intention is for evil ends, while the left's intention is for the good of all. Anyone on the right who breaks laws must be subjected to the maximum consequence. Conversely, anyone on the left should be spared any consequence at all, if possible, because the "good" they do outweighs whatever infractions they may have committed (treason, sedition, or otherwise). When someone on the right uses the same tactics that those on the left routinely use, he or she is accused of dirty tricks, right-wing conspiracies, hate, etc. Wait, let's revise that: when someone on the right *opposes* anyone or anything on the left, he or she is accused of dirty tricks, right-wing conspiracies, hate, etc.

How does a society arrive at such a juncture where such hypocrisy is tolerated? Answer: slow cultivation. With special cultural gardening tools and special flora in hand, Lefty seeds the ground of ideas, obsessively nurturing every sign of growth, obsessively fostering fruitful ventures, and obsessively pruning those that grow too wild, too early—that is to say, those wild roots that have the potential to expose the agenda too early on in the game. Regardless of these distractions, once Lefty's horticultural work is completed and the victory garden has been prepped, the time is near for the "special" flora to overtake and suffocate the healthy vegetation.

Next, we will explore the special tools, techniques, and flora Lefty uses to take ground in the battle against liberty.

Relativism

The field of leftist dreams is a culture prepped by a heavy dose of relativism. Why? Because relativism provides a vehicle by which the left can question foundational tenets and norms. With relativism in the soil, everything can be differentiated by shades of gray. In a relativistic world, there is no right or wrong, thus radical opinion and perspectives can easily wedge themselves into the cultural mainstream. Then, as soon as relativism becomes the de facto litmus test, one who continues to delineate between right and wrong is flagged as a heretic to the new order. Consequently, anyone who continues to point out the existence of right and wrong is eventually labeled as evil—no relativism there! Eventually, such "heretics" are branded as dangerous to the new order and are slotted for quarantine or preferably, elimination.

Thus is the lunacy of the left. Relativism provides a mechanism for the acceptance of leftist ideology, yet leftists *absolutely* reject anything that exposes or contradicts their ideology. Another underlying reason for pushing relativism is that Lefty wants to be the ultimate determiner of right and wrong, and ironically, how he arrives at this self-appointed appointment is via the bridge of relativism. To make matters worse, relativism is laden with cultural demise. Subsequently, the resultant transformation ends in a reversal of values. For example, in a free society, the state is subject to the individual. After transformation to a leftist society, the individual is subject to the state. Thus, the beauty of a relativistic world (to a leftist) is that everything can be redefined. What was good can be portrayed as evil and what was evil can be portrayed as good.

Inoculation

Lefty has devised an ingenious system by which the left cannot be attacked and yet grants a liberal allowance of attacks on the opposition. This *coup de raison* is accomplished by portraying a selected group as an underdog, or a victim, who is downtrodden as a direct result of, as Lefty unabashedly claims, the policies of the opposition. The extension is then made that since the selected "victim" group is underprivileged, pinned down, mistreated, and unequal, they deserve nothing more than proactive compassion, reparation, and subsidy. Anything else, even simply ignoring their "plight," is tantamount to deliberately fostering, promoting, and continuing their victim status.

The process of inoculation is characterized by repeatedly labeling the chosen group as victims. This portrayal of victimhood is typically accompanied by constantly showcasing the worst of situations and statistics that just so happen to involve a member of the "victimized" group. For example, portraying only those situations in "the chosen" are victims of a crime are highlighted. The fact that the same crime may happen to others who are not a member of the chosen group is nary reported.

Another sly tactic of inoculation is for Lefty to declare that the opposition is labeling him (Lefty), or a selected "victim" group, as inferior. There are caches of pre-constructed phrases that invariably cause immediate retreat by the opposition. For example, take the quip, "Are you questioning my patriotism?" The statement is ingenious in that it forces the opposition to admit publicly, willingly or unwillingly, that the leftist is indeed a patriot and is operating with the best interests of the country in mind. This in turn gives credence to the leftist and inoculation from the charge of being unpatriotic!

So why not say, "Yes, I do question your patriotism!"? First, few individuals have the ability to confront someone in private, never mind in a public forum. Second, most may fear the follow-up question: "Well then, who decides who is patriotic and who is not?" Before the former can even utter a word, he or she will be labeled as someone who is ready to embark on the next Stalinist purge (where millions died, administered by an individual whom the left *admires*), or even worse, accused of McCarthyism (where millions watched, administered by an individual who the left *abhors*).

On Premise

The left does their best to take control of the debate whenever possible. One of the favorite "sleight of tongue" techniques is to set up a false premise. In this manner, the debate is artificially limited to the premise. Take, for example, the issue of government waste. The two options are always put forth: does the public want higher taxes or less public safety? This is nothing but a virtual shell game. Why are the only choices higher taxes or less public safety? How about lower taxes and increased public safety? How about lower taxes and less bureaucracy? How about lower taxes and more individual disposable income? How about a whole slew of alternatives that are never asked?

A false premise usually arises in an interview format where the interviewer (host) and/or the interviewee (guest) is/are determined to push an agenda. The interviewee (guest) is directed loaded question after loaded question to give credence to the premise. If the guest obliges the host, whatever credentials the guest came with are lent to the premise. Even if the guest does not have credentials, the fact that there is one more talking head agreeing with a fabricated premise supports the premise—well, in leftist circles anyway. In any case, there are many reasons why guests on such forums are reluctant to challenge the host, and few do. This is primarily due to the fact that either the hosts and or the guests who are practicing leftists are rarely going to allow time to someone who is philosophically distant from their own viewpoint. Put it this way, whether the leftist is the guest or the host, if the leftist is challenged, they will nary be seen in that setting again—they cannot take the challenge.

Demonization

Probably the most oft-used tactic employed by the left to disable an opponent is demonization. In demonization, leftists attack their opponents (and if necessary, family members, friends, and associates) by magnifying any flaw, deed, or association, you name it, in order to sway popular opinion to break against their opponent. Demonization provides multiple, delectable outcomes for the leftist. At first, the practice of demonization clues in leftist allies in the media, and elsewhere, to ride hard on the opponent. Then, given time, as the process gathers steam, fair-weather friends peel away from the target. In the final rounds, if support for the target has eroded significantly, right or wrong, the target may be forced to retreat and choose from a list of undesirable exit strategies.

It is to this end that the left, in a methodical, step-by-step series of attacks, uses demonization to take out opposition forces. If one tactic bears unfruitful, Lefty methodically and unrelentingly moves onto another tactic. First stop on the "politics of personal destruction" tour: yesterday.

Bring up the Past

When confronted with an issue from the political right, weighing the merits and deficits of the issue are not of prime importance to leftists. No, the first order of the day is to comb the opponent's background, checking for any illegal activity (as in "grab the FBI file (or MI5 file, or FSB file, or …)." Looking for an opponent's past misdeeds and mistakes is a pleasurable event for the garden variety leftist (a process than has been known to trigger drooling among the faithful). The caveat in demonization is that the potential damage is pretty much determined by the target's political and ideological affiliation. For example, the core liberal base will give a pass to almost any activity, including treason and murder. So with liberals, such tactics are mostly ineffective. However, for those on the right, illegal activity tends to turn off the conservative law and order base. The double irony is that demonization is not used to strengthen the resolve of the leftist base to defeat the opposition on the right but to weaken the support of the conservative base for its own team member!

Now it is true that past behavior can be a predictor of future actions, but the key here is "can be." For the left, regardless of the circumstances, the past is to be used as a weapon, forged for maximum impact. As one could guess, criminal activity is the most favored because it can have the greatest impact. In this case, the desired emotional reactions are already in place for Lefty to use as a weapon, resulting in less work on the front end for Lefty.

However, for many a salivating socialist, convictions are not necessary. For that matter, neither is rehabilitation or a changed life considered a roadblock on the avenue of personal destruction. The important part for the leftist, more or less, is *if* one has ever been charged. Everything else is icing on the cake. Important facts that exonerate a person can be ignored, and all contexts can be thrown out the window. All salacious details will be magnified, twisted as much as possible, and then broadcast for their maximum effect. If the allegation was twenty years ago, Lefty wants to make you think it just happened yesterday. All the details are made fresh, released, and re-released time and time again to keep the story buoyant in the media. Or even better: if the dirt is perceived to be truly damaging, the left wing political-media complex will hold on to the information until the time they deem appropriate—like the weekend before an election.

On the other side of the spectrum, when the right attempts to use this tactic, it rarely works. Remember, the goal of demonization is to put distance between the *leadership of the opposition* and *its own base*. Such accusations do not turn off the core base of the left: to core leftists, most convictions are bogus. In their mind, cop killers should be set free and unrepentant domestic terrorists are deserving of commutation or pardon.

The conundrum for the right lies in the difference in philosophies. On the political right, actual crimes are what they are. Otherwise, one is free to think and associate as one wishes, as long one does not infringe upon the rights of others. For the left, however, a politically incorrect thought life may very well be the highest crime in the land; speaking freely about what one thinks is akin to taking a stand against the political body.

Looking closer at this phenomenon, it appears that the act that constitutes the most egregious leftist crime boils down to the exercise of free thought because ultimately, on the left, thinking for oneself is considered deadly anathema. Why, free thinking may lead to free speech, and likewise, free speech may lead to life, liberty, and the pursuit of happiness!

Therefore, to prevent such an outbreak, leftist rank and file must drink the Kool-Aid, without question. If not, they too are then subject to demonization. In the same manner that Lefty investigates the background of an opponent, he will also, sometimes simultaneously, investigate the background of a comrade. The purpose is to have an insurance policy in the event that a party member exhibits symptoms of independent thought. Should this occur, such antithetical notions will require a prompt exorcism. Of course, the outcome for a target who is a leftist is generally different than that of a target on the right. Possibly due to the "honor among fascists" code, the process is much more discrete, generally void of dragging the fellow comrade through the public channels. Usually the process is subtle and simple: one of the faithful members drops by to remind the wayward party member of his or her past discrepancies and how it will be beneficial to keep them there (in the past) (as in "We grabbed your FBI (MI5, FSB …) file too … shhhhhhhhhhh …").

Is it not ironic that the very people who promote early release for dangerous offenders, conjugal visits for inmates, and weekend furloughs for dangerous criminals are the same people that have no sense of forgiveness or willingness to overlook the past of their political enemies? It always comes down to one thing: power and control. Don't ever forget that.

Trip on the Details

So what if the past does not pan out? The next step is to look for any procedural errors up to, and including, honest mistakes made by the target—in other words, verification that the target is indeed operating as a human being. Take the example of a public persona who does not remember to register to vote, or registers in the wrong place, or shows up to vote in the wrong voting location. Initially, there is an "outcry" (translation: leftist generated media storm) to call into question the judgment of the person. The generated "public" questioning that follows usually goes like this: "If we cannot trust them to act appropriately in their own private affairs, how can we trust them to speak on the issues that face our (fill in the blank—'city,' 'state,' or 'country')?"

The incident is then fanned ad nauseam in the public forum with the hope of eroding the target's judgment and persona. At the same time, political leaders on the right, wandering aimlessly in the media wilderness, ignore the story *and* the attack. Why? Possibly because many on the right have this silly notion that all are human and that such mistakes do not amount to anything of substance, much less one's overall character. To the right, such discrepancies do not generally merit time or attention. There also appears to exist a "There but for the grace of God go I" sentiment among those on the right. To those on the left, this type of outlook is seen as senseless folly, not to mention the acknowledgement that God actually exists. To the left, one must accuse and slander one's opponent from any angle, substance or no substance. Winning is everything!

Now, once a procedural error is discovered, legal lefties scour the legal code at local, state, and federal level to find if a letter, even a punctuation mark, of the law fell to the ground. If anything remotely related is found, they lick their chops and call the nearest prosecutor, whom they demand open up a "full" investigation. Of course, if the prosecutor is not a leftist ally and the investigation outcome is not deemed satisfactory, the left will open up a second negative campaign front on the prosecutor. To the left, what the target actually did or did not do is not important; the opposition is automatically guilty of the high crime of impeding the progress of the leftist steamroller. On the left, guilt is predetermined—investigations, prosecutions, and verdicts are mere post-event procedural formalities.

Character analysis

If no illegal activity or procedural error can be found, the process becomes more creative. Truly, at the core of all these tactics is character assassination. So how the left arrives at that goal does not really matter, which leads us to the next tactic: perform a microanalysis of the behavioral characteristics or character nuances, and then exploit those that can be magnified or presented in a negative tone. This tactic fits in nicely with a core talent on the left: crafting messages to paint mental pictures and then starting the buzz over the airwaves.

The procedure usually starts with a word that is used over and over again for the purpose of exaggerating a trait that is mostly undeserved. For example, the target may be said to have a certain "swagger." At this point, the buzz is started and *the match is lit.* Then, from one single label, a progression is developed and spelled out for the public. The word "swagger" is associated with someone who is cocky. Someone who is cocky does not seek the counsel of others. Someone who does not seek the counsel of others makes decisions on their own. Someone who makes decisions on their own is living in their own world. Someone who is living on their own is socially, mentally, and ideologically isolated. Someone who is ideologically isolated has thoughts no one can know or predict. This could be a madman! And if that person is in charge of a country, world war could be just around the corner! At this nadir, and after much fanning the flames, the buzz is raging and the little match fire has become a media firestorm.

Public conversation will take place over time, with an uncanny pace. First the association of linking the individual with the "swagger" characteristic will be sowed and nurtured until it self-perpetuates in the media. This is not hard to do when you have willing accomplices in the media who know when to carry the ball and hand it off since they are on the same side as Lefty. Then, once it is "established" that the target has a *swagger*, the new media-created persona is expanded upon and referred to over and over again. Fait accompli!

Next, with the *franken* persona created, the target will forever be linked with the *franken* traits. From that point on, every statement, every move, and every proposal is questioned. And now, because we are told that "we now know" how the target operates, the target is labeled unstable or untrustworthy. This is the fantasy-to-reality world in which the leftist successfully operates: pure fiction becomes accepted common knowledge.

Accusation

What if nothing sticks? Make a wild accusation! Lie! Once one is accused or libeled, one must defend every past, present, and future action. In a way, accusation is an alternative method of taking the opposition out of the game. Some become so politically wounded that they never fully recover. Although leftists love to portray themselves otherwise, being mean-spirited and outright fanatical is acceptable and is actually required for promotion through the ranks. Contrary to popular opinion, true empathy is nary to be discovered on the left.

What if the person (a.k.a. the target) is near sainthood? Easy, Lefty is a master at manipulating the rules of the game. He ensures that no one on the right will ever be portrayed as "good enough" by constantly raising the bar of behavior for the right, while at the same time disposing of any bar for the left. Those on the right should always remember: laws are enacted by *those on the right* to exact punishment for the purpose of deterring and preventing criminal behavior; laws are enacted by *those on the left* to exact punishment for the purpose of deterring and preventing oppositional behavior!

Demonization is the constant eroding of the target's persona, until image rehabilitation becomes difficult or even impossible. Yet the very practice should cause the public to pause and ask: "What about the issue?" When the public at large learns to put aside the sins or supposed sins of the target and force the spotlight to refocus on the issues, Lefty will be dealt a huge blow. Not only will it cause inspection to be focused where it should be, but it will also encourage others who, because of the fear of demonization, are intimidated into silence.

Offense Offensive

Leftists love to rant and rave about how an opponent has offended them and their sensibilities. The goal is to coerce the target to apologize for something that is usually innocuous. Then, once the target apologizes, some form or reparative action is required to quell the hyper-traumatized sensibilities of the offended. Next, soon after the apology for the first "offense" is issued, it will not be long until new charges of offense are brought to bear. Summarily, once the target is sufficiently labeled as a serial egregious aggressor, prevailing wisdom dictates that the target "must be" consistently corrected.

Once again, one must jettison logic and common sense. The offense is typically drummed up or exaggerated to make the target look like a monster in the public view. And true to form, the goal is not for the target to see the error of his or her ways; quite the contrary. The goal is to paint an unflattering portrait of the target in the public space, and more importantly, condition the target to become a chronic apologizer and to keep the target constantly on defense. The target, wanting to move on or get out of the headlines, obliges by apologizing and usually some form of payoff, playing right into Lefty's hand. The public, after witnessing the apology and "outreach," then assumes that the target was wrong. After all, why apologize? After a series of apologies, the public makes the next logical conclusion that the target really has some problems. All the while, Lefty sits back and watches the process with glee.

Fear

Leftists are well aware that they must use the stick as much as they use the carrot. The stick they use, a negative motivator in this sense, is fear. It is not the fear of intimidation used to silence opposition (however, that type of fear is used as well) but the fear of dire predictions, the fear of uncertainty, and the fear of apocryphal outcomes. For example:

The world has about ten years before man's impact on the environment will be irreversible. We must act now!

Implication: unless you participate and influence others to participate, our world, our very future, is in peril. It is imperative upon all who live and breathe in the world, not only to join in the effort to step out and fight global warming but to also influence others. All must participate, or all are doomed to a global failure! Hence, the herd effect: the world needs to move leftward to ensure survival of the planet. Conveniently, should the issue dissipate, Lefty is ready to conveniently forget the issue wholesale and is unashamedly ready to take credit for sounding the alarm and preventing it from happening!

Again, Lefty uses fear and uncertainty to mask what the public should really fear: his true fascist intentions of taking control of everyone's life. *Clarification point*: the tactics of the left should not be mistaken with legitimate movements with legitimate reasons. A legitimate political figure may inform the populace of upcoming fearful events that are sincerely believed to be true. In such a case, the public is obviously being warned for their own benefit.

The question then arises: how does one tell the difference? The key is this: leftists cannot generally back up their claims. And more importantly, leftists always want to extract something of value from you: rights, values, and money. Besides, if there truly is an actual crisis, the left does not want it resolved. Solving crises does not help Lefty in any way (more on that later). On the other hand, verifiable leaders will typically have common sense reasoning, historical facts, plain integral numbers, or all of the above to back up their premise.

It should be obvious by now that the left is constantly subjecting the unwary public to relentless psychological warfare. The premise, however sinister, is that constant psychological conditioning will eventually result in a consistent Pavlovian response. To this end, the left's goal is to program who and what society is offended by, who and what society is against, and ultimately, who and what society thinks is good and evil.

Unfortunately for humanity, such a scheme has been proven to work time and time again. Whether conscious of the fact or not, whether we want to acknowledge it or not, it is possible for a society to be subjected to a message that will actually make individuals reject their basic liberties. Yes, that is correct: actually make individuals' own minds work against themselves and their loved ones.

This cultural ruse is done purposefully and with reasoned intent: Lefty likes to put the psychological restraints on first, because later on in the game, it makes it so much easier to put on the physical restraints.

Immersion

"The price of freedom is eternal vigilance."
—Thomas Jefferson

L earning a second language is truly an enriching experience. Even if done for purely academic reasons, the experience is well worth it. However, anyone serious about learning a second language soon understands that a classroom environment can only touch upon the reality of living, thinking, and speaking in the native lingual environment. Therefore, to fully embrace a second language, aspiring linguists engage in what is called an immersion experience. An immersion experience is where one travels to the region of the lingual interest to live, eat, and breathe the language, the culture, and the people. The ultimate goal is to integrate into the culture and function as a native speaker. In the end, not only does one learn a different language, but one learns different perspectives as well. After such a rewarding experience, rarely does one walk away without being culturally and intellectually richer than before.

Enter stage left. In a twisted version of the immersion experience, leftists plant themselves inside a target culture. Their purpose is not to soak up the target culture's customs and ways but to infect it with leftist language, culture, and perspective. In this sense, the left practices *reverse immersion*. Sadly, following such an experience, the target society is left intellectually, spiritually, and materially poorer than before.

Immersion is the stage, in leftist encroachment, where Lefty expands beyond the academic setting and enters into the practical world. Lefty, understand, is fully aware that mere words and tactics are not powerful enough to seize the cultural castle. As well, he is fully aware that an all-out assault is a high-risk venture. Therefore, the only safe alternative is a slow infiltration of the target culture—a feat that is primarily accomplished by picking organizations and positions within organizations, that will yield the greatest return and simultaneously offer the least resistance. Then, once they have a foothold, infiltrating other areas of the cultural castle becomes easier. Eventually, if the process is allowed to continue to a tipping point, remaining holdouts will fall like dominoes.

There is a phenomenon that occurs after some initial success in the process of reverse immersion: society is fooled into thinking that those sectors that have been infiltrated are naturally leftist. The mirage could not be further from the truth. Take actors and journalists, for example. Those drawn to either profession are not necessarily liberal. The fact that these professions come to be peppered with liberals is done by artificial means. Here is how it happens: first, Lefty worms his way in and becomes ensconced in influential positions. From that point on, those actors and journalists who show promise are promoted; those who display a love for God, family, and country are marginalized. So, the message is clear: be the good boy or girl that Uncle Lefty wants you to be and your career is a smooth upward trajectory. On the other hand, show any signs of conservatism and you will be the receiver of bit parts and bad assignments. As a result of this practice, most conservatives are gradually forced out of the business to seek success elsewhere. Thereafter, political correctness becomes so pervasive in the ranks that it naturally prevents entry of any independent-minded newcomers.

Reverse immersion, which is nothing more than infiltration of an entire culture, is similar to the practice of "salting." In the construction industry, *salting* refers to the method that unions employ to infiltrate and unionize a nonunion company (interestingly, nonunion companies are known as "merit shops"). The salting process begins when union management "encourages" union personnel to get hired on at a merit shop. Once hired on, the job of the union's double agent is to slow down work, cause problems, and basically muck up the works—all in the name of "fair" wages. At the same time, the undercover union hack espouses the wonderful life of a union member to the field of potential converts. All the while, the merit shop may not know that such mischief is being engineered or when discovered, from where it may be coming. Nice, "fair" individuals to deal with, huh?

Just as in salting, the left infiltrates many institutions and segments in society: legislative, judicial, educational, business, media, finance—you name it. Take the judicial system, for example. Operatives (a.k.a. salting agents) quietly insert themselves into key places without the public ever knowing an agenda is afoot. In due time, when the left has a case that comes to trial, it may just so happen that there is a sympathetic ear sitting on the bench or a friend in the prosecutor's office, or both. This explains some of the nonsensical decisions and cases that are handed down—evidence that the system has been infiltrated.

Expanding leftist infiltration to a macro scale, one sees that once enough institutions and segments in society have been sufficiently compromised, leftist operatives work together to embolden an agenda that encompasses multiple segments of society. That way, infiltrated segments can symbiotically abet each other in pushing the agenda forward. For example, the media and legislative sectors may collude to further one or the other's pet agenda. Sound too improbable? Never underestimate the left's ability to infiltrate and influence a culture. Such collusion happens constantly and as mentioned previously, does not have to be an organized conspiracy. It is simply the left obsessively doing what the left is maniacally driven to do: constantly herding the populace to the leftist ideal.

Now, once a critical mass of infiltration has occurred, the left has a much easier time exacting devious designs on society. These schemes typically have a predictable pattern that can be summarized as follows:

1. There is a "problem" that is promoted as a "crisis" of urgent attention. Every "crisis" needs to be solved, unless you have no desire to save the planet *or* the children.

2. The leftist solution is virtually the only one proffered. Other faux solutions may be displayed only for the purpose of being shot down to make the original one seem like the best option. Practical solutions or contradicting evidence are ridiculed, ignored, and/or branded negatively.

3. Accept the leftist solution, "crisis" is over, and as a bonus, your conscience is officially cleared.

4. Do not accept the leftist solution and the obsessive left will look for other ways to enable the agenda.

Or another twist on the same theme:

1. There is a group of people with a problem, and that group is promoted as "victims." If your conscience is not tortured day and night, you must be evil or ignorant.

2. The leftist solution is basically the only solution proffered. Any opposing solution is given a negative branding that includes the word "hate."

3. Accept the leftist solution, and the group will not be victimized anymore. Your conscience is now officially cleared.

4. Do not accept the leftist solution and the left will look for other ways to enable the agenda, or to use the politically correct phraseology: "empower the victims."

Of course, the above is a great oversimplification. Through the course of the public discussion, there may be points and counterpoints, resistance, and even defeats. But the goal is basically the same: drive the agenda to universal acceptance. And while we are touching on the notion of universal acceptance, a clarification is in order. *Universal acceptance*, at least for the left, does not mean universal agreement. On the contrary, qualification for universal acceptance means that leftist ideas are "universally accepted" due to legal enforcement, misinformation, or public apathy!

This leftist concept of problem solving cannot be stated enough. Do not be fooled into the notion that the leftist aim is to really solve the crisis or protect the victim. The only goal is to consolidate power. If the crisis is solved or the victim protected, that is just an aberrant, random outcome. In practice, too much actual problem solving is a bad thing for Lefty. If there aren't any problems, then why should society stray from the status quo? On the contrary: the more *crises or victims*, real, imagined, or fomented, the better. Lefty uses crises and victims (real, imagined, or fomented) to drive society right into his trap.

Take the debate on socialized medicine. Obviously the push from the left is not a quest to provide health care for everyone. On the contrary, it is nothing more than a power grab of the health care industry and, simultaneously, to ensure increased dependence on government; to bring all sectors under one scepter of power: health care, financial, industrial, etc. Lefty knows that he cannot grab the whole national pie at once, so he takes it piecemeal, bit by bit. Should he be successful in garnering control of one, Lefty will move on to the next sector. Today the debate may be healthcare, tomorrow the debate moves on to the financial sector, and then ... get the picture?

Leftist stealth takeover is just like war (in fact, it is a war on liberty). For example, during the outset of World War II , as country after country fell under the Nazi offensive, the ability for neighboring countries to resist became harder and harder as they lost their old neighbors and gained a demonstrably hostile one. The remaining countries were now left to renegotiate terms with a new regime. Given the propensity of invasion by the Nazis (*national* socialists, by the way), the remaining countries were much more agreeable than before because a new reality had presented itself: survival!

So it is the same with the classic leftist offensive. Just like dominos, they knock over one sector of society at a time, consolidating power until there aren't any dominos standing.

Applying this to the health care model, just consider independent economic sectors that deal with a federalized health care industry. These sectors will have to adapt and change if they want to remain viable. Why? A federalized health care system will have the legislative backing to punish (*leftspeak* translation: "regulate") those sectors that do not agree to new conformities. Before, what was an exchange between two free market sectors now becomes an exchange between an oppressive government with legal enforcement powers and a free market sector—the very type of entity an oppressive government despises! Guess who has the advantage?

But before embarking on such an enormous undertaking, there is a seminal question that leftists must ponder: which domino to knock over first? Health care, as attractive as it is, is much too large to tackle at first run. Thus, they wisely scout the cultural landscape for those institutions that offer minimal resistance and yet have a great potential for influence. Naturally, since leftists are gifted control freaks, they are drawn to a vehicle that allows them to sell their message. The obvious and first candidate is the national soapbox, otherwise known collectively as the media.

The Media Realm

The media is truly the gateway drug for leftists. Not only is it used to sow the leftist message into the national soil, but it is also used to control the flow of information, to determine what is news and what isn't, to promote what is acceptable science and what isn't, to declare what is moral and what isn't, and to decide what is entertainment and what isn't. Additionally, the media is used as a platform to intimidate and softly blackmail government officials, business leaders, and the like, with implied questions such as, "Would you like positive or negative coverage?" or "Highlight, or spotlight?" Armed with these powers, the media (in leftist hands) has the ability to influence others to fall in line or be subject to celluloid intimidation.

News

The news media is probably the most important and powerful of all media and probably the most powerful weapon of the left. Because the news media is the public's primary connection to world events, it wields tremendous influence over issues that impact our lives. And in this 24/7 connected world, it may be even more indispensable.

This makes the news media ground zero in the war for the hearts and minds of the populace.

With the news media in leftists' hands, there is a constant drum beat of diversion. Imagine failed social programs being in the headlines every day. It would not take long before the problem was resolved. Instead, such information is kept under wraps. Goal *numero uno* for a leftist-controlled media is to hide the leftist agenda (i.e., minimization) from the public, while keeping the issues that the left wants to advance in the forefront (i.e., maximization). They want the populace to always be thinking about the latest leftist-generated crisis. The entire purpose is to keep you from reading, listening to, or focusing on issues that matter, and most importantly, to keep you from focusing on your liberties while they quietly steal away with them.

Get it out of your mind that such individuals are reasonable, who, if presented with the facts, would change their mind. They are supposed to be the *de facto* fact finders! Likewise, do not ever believe that such types will be allies of freedom, for they only have a hidden agenda: infiltrating the news media with leftist operatives and influencing the culture.

But alas, this is nothing new. Socialists have always known that it is critically important to occupy the echelons of the media industry if they were to influence the masses. The great fascists of old all understood and exploited the power of the media. Note the following, courtesy of the archives of Stalin, *prima facie* evidence of the left's natural attraction to the media:

> *"One might ask why the KGB would recruit a journalist like Stone, then an editorial writer for the New York Post, with no access to government or industrial secrets. In fact, the KGB recruited a great many journalists. A 1941 internal KGB summary report broke down the occupations of Americans working for the spy agency in the prior decade. Twenty-two were journalists, a profession outnumbered only by engineers (forty-nine) and dwarfing economists (four) and professors (eight). While journalists rarely had direct access to technical secrets or classified documents in the way engineers, scientists, or*

government officials did, the espionage enterprise encompasses more than the classic spy who physically steals a document.

The KGB recruited journalists in part for their access to inside information and sources on politics and policy, insights into personalities, and confidential and non-public information that never made it into published stories. Certain journalistic working habits also lent themselves to intelligence tasks. By profession, journalists ask questions and probe; what might seem intrusive or suspect if done by anyone else is their normal modus operandi. Consequently, the KGB often used journalists as talent spotters for persons who did have access to sensitive information, and made use of them to gather background information that would help in evaluating candidates for recruitment.

The flexibility of their work also made journalists desirable as couriers and agent handlers (the liaisons between KGB officers and their American sources). There was also much less risk that a journalist having contact with a government official or engineer would attract the attention of security officials than would a KGB officer under Soviet diplomatic cover. And even if security officials did notice such a meeting, it would be much easier to provide a benign explanation for contact with a pesky American journalist than with a Soviet diplomat. Additionally, the KGB could use journalists for "active measures"—the planting of a story in the press or giving a slant to a story that served KGB goals." [8]

Do not be surprised if in the media, this very day, there exist individuals who are followers of such ilk, longing for the leftist paradise, knowing they cannot come out of the closet just yet. In the meantime, they will do their best to deliver the world to us on their terms.

When it comes to news, *caveat emptor*!

---

8   http://www.commentarymagazine.com/viewarticle.cfm/i-f--stone--soviet-agent-case-closed-15120)

Entertainment

The entertainment industry offers Lefty a multifaceted front, where any venue for entertainment can be used as a vehicle for socialist dribble. Through movies, documentaries, plays, musical productions, children's shows, cartoons, talk shows, etc., entertainment has the ability to interweave a message into a program that is tailor-made for a target audience. What more could a leftist ask for?

Entertainment under leftist influence employs strong imagery and verbal innuendo to subtly impress a central theme on the mind. As is standard in any propagandist script, emotion is heavy and facts are hard to come by. The classical leftist theme is a story where traditional values and stereotypes associated with those values are portrayed in a negative light, whereas leftist ideologies and practices are held up as virtuous.

And of course, the same message is delivered over and over, in production after production, differentiated only by sporting a different title and façade each time. The goal is that with each successive iteration of the dogma, the propaganda will finally settle into the cultural psyche and make the populace question long-held beliefs about their country, their values, and ultimately, themselves. Even more sinister is when the prime target is the up and coming generation, for whom Lefty has one aim: to fill their youthful mass of uninitiated neurons with leftist propaganda and stake a claim in their mind before the truth can make its way there.

Another favorite vehicle, edutainment (education in the form of entertainment), also assists Lefty in his holistic effort to undermine society. Edutainment productions, such as documentaries, are littered with phrases such as "scientists are not sure why, but they theorize" or "scientists think" or "most *(fill in the blank)ologists* agree." In these "educational" presentations, the audience is unknowingly (yet purposefully) driven to a preordained conclusion. In production after production, the same "concepts" are repeated over and over again, reinforced by "experts." The result is a living room audience left to accept the premises put forth or take the "indefensible" position of disagreeing with the "mountain of evidence" and the plethora of *accepted* "facts"!

For example, decades ago, evolution was presented as theory. Today, evolution is presented over and over as fact, even though nothing dramatically in favor of evolution has been discovered. In fact, if anything, information contradicting findings has come to light. But because such evidence does not support the underlying argument for leftist hegemony, it is kept as far as possible from the lights, the camera, and the action. So let's be clear—not all educational documentaries are biased. The problem is, once Lefty infiltrates the ranks, truth is harder to come by.

To make matters worse, modern living may act as a catalyst for the electronic indoctrination, for most of us watch these presentations insulated in our living rooms, while expert after expert with impressive letters trailing after their last names are paraded in front of us. As they tell us about places we have never been or things that we have never seen or experiments we have never tried, is it possible that we may wonder subconsciously: am I, without impressive degrees or accolades, qualified to say anything? Ironically, reaching such a conclusion is the result of prior leftist psychological conditioning!

The Government Realm

If the media is the gateway drug, then government, the seat of power, is the ultimate aphrodisiac. Government is where the action is, where the levers of control exist, and is ultimately where Lefty wants to be. There are three main areas that Lefty worms his way into: administrative, appointed, and elected.

Infiltration via the administrative side is simple: get hired. It does not matter what the position, for the idea is to get in and work one's way up the ladder or, at the very least, become a support system by surrounding the seats of influence. After all, one does not have to be in a leadership position to affect outcome; those who support the leader can have significant influence as well.

Appointed positions, being more visible than the administrative positions of government, are naturally somewhat more involved when it comes to infiltration. The decision to appoint someone is usually left up to an elected official or a combination thereof and typically has some element of public awareness. Regardless, most appointments escape public notice, even high-profile ones, especially when there is a complicit media.

Elected positions are the most difficult to infiltrate, mainly due to the highly visible nature of being an office holder. Regardless, Lefty has a proven plan to successfully infiltrate these positions as well. This is where a complicit media is extremely helpful.

Once leftists are sprinkled throughout the government, the ship naturally steers in one direction: left. Consequently, reversing course becomes more difficult as leftist infiltration takes it toll.

Aiming for the Children

Special mention needs to be made about a special sector of government: education. The most insidious, despicable, and unconscionable acts of the left are the campaigns to corrupt the young, the innocent, and the naïve: our children. And the most evil of all leftist infiltrations is the one of education, because adults have the ability to discern, even when they are being deceived, but not so with children. Children do not have enough time or experience to develop the faculties to discern deception from truth. On top of that, children are sponges when it comes to information. Lefty takes full advantage of these factors and infiltrates the education system to prepare (as in cooking) their minds for blind obedience to the leftist creed. The goal is to psychologically condition and train children to elicit the "appropriate" responses, so when the children come of age, they can assist Lefty in taking over the world that their parents ran.

This is why universal preschool education for all is pushed—earlier indoctrination! This is the impetus behind so-called sex education. What it really amounts to is a cover to promote various agendas via the education system. Think about it. All the species on the planet—elephants, gnus, walruses, bats, rats, and rabbits—manage to propagate just fine. But we humans, supposed higher forms of intelligence, need reproductive education. *Side note: "It" is never "for the children," but employing such phrasing will get buy-in from the public.*

There is nothing new about this concept—we just need to peer back to the Nazi (national *socialist*) regime of Adolf Hitler. By the time the National Socialist Party was ready for war, the Hitler Youth had been prepped and indoctrinated. The brainwashing was so bad that parents were afraid of their own children, for fear that their own children would turn them in to the authorities. Make no mistake: the left has dead aim on our children today, just as it has in years gone by. If there is a rescue effort that is needed more than any other, it is to rescue our children from the grip of the leftists in the educational system.

The Financial Realm

Ascending to a seat of power requires money and more importantly, the power that money carries with it. Although political power is always the ultimate goal, wealth can influence many an individual and fund many an agenda. With financial and business institutions infiltrated, wealth can be redirected to favored leftist causes; likewise, the power associated with money can be used to promote leftist policies.

Many a financial foundation is a coveted target for takeover by the left. Because these foundations and their kind quietly operate in the backdrop of society, they make the perfect vehicle for a stealth takeover. Now it just so happens that once leftist agents are entrenched inside, *coincidentally*, receivers of grants are gently pressured to make policy changes to conform to the new master's wishes. At the same time, *coincidentally*, the back door of the institution is opened for leftist applicants who, apprised of their comrades' new digs, apply and, *coincidentally*, receive express approval for their projects.

In the more visible business world, leftist minions use similar tactics to engulf the host. From challenging traditional norms, diverting corporate funds to leftist causes, to hiring fellow sympathizers to form a power block—all is done in the name of controlling the power and influence of the business. Once a business has been infiltrated, promotion and other forms of career enhancements are primarily based on knowledge and practice of leftist correctness. Those who are in the fold and display promise receive the help of the invisible hand. Consequently, the business will never operate near its potential since merit and ethics are trumped and muted by political correctness.

The Religious Realm

The last stronghold of values, the religious realm, is the *piece de resistance* for the left. Strong with customs and tenets that predate most modern countries, religion is a natural roadblock to societal deconstruction. Note that religion is the only realm discussed so far that is considered to reach beyond the earthly plane; religion defers to a power higher than man, a notion that Lefty cannot stand. After all, in Lefty's mind, he is to be the only arbiter of all, not some celestial being he cannot control! This is a concept that is even extremely maddening for Lefty: a supreme being whom the faithful hold as the highest authority!

Because of the obvious chasm between value systems, the infiltration of religion would seem to be nearly impossible. However, Lefty is adept at manipulating orthodoxy and summarily bridging the orthodox with the heretical. First, the recipe calls for plain, old-fashioned infiltration. In other words, say what needs to be said and do what needs to be done to get in the door. Then, through doctrinal incrementalism, selectively question and methodically water down the tenets of old. The end result is a religion that withers on the vine as it loses flavor and traditional adherents—a brave new quorum consisting of an old, fading membership and new, hostile homesteaders. Not surprisingly, the only new membership typically attracted is other leftist adherents. As this process continues and the institution becomes laden with a critical mass of leftist agents, a series of doctrinal initiatives magically spring up to question the sacred traditions. In concert with other efforts, a constant drumbeat of obsessive rants against the traditions are sounded until the old guard simply tires out, caves in, or is replaced with *progressive saints*.

One may think that wrestling for control of the media, the government, the financial sector, and the religious institutions would be enough. And yet, it is not, especially for the obsessive-driven control freaks on the left. Always unsatisfied, they continually attempt to infiltrate every organization and institution in the land, even if the organization's or institution's precepts are in stark contrast to the leftist ideals. Whether it is the ladies' tea, youth groups, environmental groups, or any other interest groups, Lefty wants to have universal reach, for all of these groups have a hierarchy and in a sense, a captive audience. And Lefty wants to be in control, wherever possible. Under leftist assault, many a group founded on noble principles winds up being a front for the socialist power struggle. Sadly, a good part of the membership of these groups is never even aware that they have been infiltrated and are being manipulated.

Once burrowed inside these groups, Lefty begins to deconstruct any traditional element that supports the ideals of life, liberty, and the pursuit of happiness. Once in control of enough of these groups, Lefty is able to saturate every corner of the culture with their terms, their language, and their dictates while asphyxiating anything that opposes or contradicts leftist tenets. That way, leftist ideology eventually becomes (or appears to become) to be the universal standard. This predicament leaves one to silently ask: "Where can I turn? These beliefs are everywhere." Get the picture?

After a successful immersion, when Lefty is firmly entrenched inside the cultural hall, he begins to overturn the banquet tables. While the populace at large is wondering why the country is going in the wrong direction, leftist infiltrators are quietly dismantling the foundations of a free society, brick by brick. While society becomes more complacent to the newly fabricated "norms," leftists carefully comb the institutions to remove any vestige of the old, stable order. Any reflection of standards, individuals, or institutions and organizations that might serve as inspirations to liberty are discredited or snuffed out so that the masses are not reminded of that which made them free. Likewise, the left replaces ideas that they consider "heretical" with new ones that reinforce the new order.

Sounds highly coordinated and conspiratorial, but it just only has to be a *concerted effort*. For leftists, working in unison comes naturally—leftist infiltration is a holistic approach that feeds on free societies until the freedoms are dissolved. When a society is wasting away through leftist incremental encroachment, the tipping point is nearing—the point when the parasite slowly begins to digest the host.

The Siege

"A nation can survive its fools, and even the ambitious. But it cannot survive treason from within. An enemy at the gates is less formidable, for he is known and he carries his banners openly. But the traitor moves among those within the gate freely, his sly whispers rustling through all the galleys, heard in the very hall of government itself. For the traitor appears not a traitor—he speaks in the accents familiar to his victims, and wears their face and their garment, and he appeals to the baseness that lies deep in the hearts of all men. He rots the soul of a nation—he works secretly and unknown in the night to undermine the pillars of a city—he infects the body politic so that it can no longer resist. A murderer is less to be feared."
—Cicero, 42 B.C.

Once the pillars of old have been infiltrated by leftists, the time to entirely compromise the traditional infrastructure begins. "The fix," as they say, "is in the works." This may explain why the left touts itself with the *progressive* moniker. The left is progressive, all right—just like a disease that metastasizes throughout the cultural body.

Once infiltration reaches critical mass (that is, "diversity" has run its course), the target society is prepped for the final stages. In these last stages, Lefty permanently jams the gears by methodically eroding the stalwart principles that built the very society in which, ironically, Lefty lives and thrives. Such hypocrisy raises a question: why would financially successful leftists want to ruin the very society in which their wealth was made possible? Answer: because their insane drive has nothing to do with money; it has to do with *power and control, power and control, power and control.* Having wealth, besides providing a great cover, doesn't necessarily change a leftist. Money only serves to enable lefties, who just so happen to be wealthy, to enact their plans with greater speed and success.

So, when the magical tipping point for the target society has been reached, leftist fangs begin to reveal themselves and the diabolical plan goes into overdrive. Leftist subversives in different sectors now easily and casually abet each other. In this final stage, where leftists are entrenched throughout the culture, the media isn't necessarily the de facto starting point to promote an agenda. Now agendas can be initiated from anywhere: government, financial institutions, religious denominations, interest groups, or a combination thereof. With other fellow travelers throughout the spectrum, the media can now passively function as the initiator, the mediator, the messenger, or the cheerleader. Subsequently, news forums expand beyond the simple promoting of leftist programs to gradually evolving to serve other purposes. Freed from having to totally conceal the light of the leftist candle, they become group therapy, public confessionals (with absolution), and open strategy sessions for the left.

It is at this tipping point where an unhealthy collusion of entities assists each other in tightening the noose around society's neck. And even though the left is well entrenched and well positioned, it is understood by most operatives that movement should continue to remain in stealth mode. After all, it has worked so far! Sure, once in while, a radical who can't hold it in any longer will stray off the plantation and reveal his or her true intentions and embarrass the movement—life happens! Generally, however, it is understood that it is imperative for the cultural giant to remain asleep during the operation, at least until the cultural giant has been sufficiently disarmed and is unable to stop the procedure.

That way, during this delicate operation, it will appear to the average citizen that hope still abounds and Lefty's ultimate goals are perceived as ridiculously unattainable. Yet regardless of public perception, Lefty will plod undaunted on the steady course quietly, procedurally, and effectively. As has been duly noted, leftists are not easily deterred and will constantly and obsessively push ahead. Setbacks are expected: the process of two steps forward with one step back is considered a decent exchange rate.

Conversely, leftists become visibly rabid when any ground already claimed is threatened, almost to the point of blowing their cover. Compromise and bipartisanship are not part of the leftist DNA. To a leftist, compromise and bipartisanship means both sides agree to implement *their* plan. To that end, to assist in their diabolical aims, the left employs a set of simple but highly effective tactics.

Incrementalism

If someone were to say to you, "Today I am going to raid your bank account and take half of your life savings," you would most likely spring into action to protect your savings, understanding that there was a clear and present danger. However, on the promise of a better world for you and others, how would you react if that same person were to say: "We will require you to pay your fair share, a mere fraction of your income, to sustain a better world for all."? Perhaps, you might not be so alarmed or defensive, even if the end result were an outcome worse than the former.

In the former method, your life savings are confiscated all at once. In the latter, your life savings are confiscated over a lifetime in comparatively small increments. Now, to make matters worse, suppose that same small payment is *incrementally* increased over the course of time in minute amounts, insignificant by themselves, yet adding up to a significant sum over time. Suppose this is done to the point where, by the time the latter is well under way, you will have had more than three-quarters of your life savings confiscated. The injury is even worse if you never realize what was really happening until it is too late.

The difference between the two methods is that one put you on immediate alarm, whereas the other made you stand down and bleed slowly. In the end, there is a greater result for the antagonist in the latter: your savings are confiscated without incurring immediate retaliation, there is access to do it again and again, and there is a modicum of control (i.e., manipulative power) over you and yours for a lifetime. In essence, the latter is akin to a bank robber convincing a bank manager to hand over the money in comparatively insignificant amounts over time versus taking it immediately by force, with all the *unnecessary* mayhem and injury that could result. This is a prime example of incrementalism (and taxes!): the antagonist puts the target at ease, who is then willingly and slowly robbed in a civil manner. Note: this form of theft is not just limited to money, for it can be applied to rights, values, you name it.

Another illustration of incrementalism is the classic story about a frog in a pot of water. As the story goes, place a frog in a pot of hot water and the frog will immediately jump out. However, place a frog in a pot of water at room temperature and the frog will most likely feel right at home. Then slowly, slowly, heat up the water a few degrees. Let some time pass and let the frog get used to the new temperature. The relaxing frog either does not notice or ignores the small, incremental environmental changes. Repeat the process over and over, increasing the heat incrementally and then waiting while the frog acclimates to the new temperature. Eventually, the frog will boil to death. This gruesome and cruel death is due to the fact that frogs can only sense big changes in temperature, not small, *incremental* changes. Turn it up to hot immediately and the frog is on to you. Turn it up gradually, *incrementally*, and his life is yours.

The same is true of society: most of us do not notice, or we simply just ignore small, incremental cultural changes. Just like the frog, such changes appear insignificant and would actually be fine if they were of the organic variety. For example, general clothing styles change and are different today than they were just half a century ago. This type of change is just a natural societal shift. Leftists, on the other hand, have a goal, and that goal consists of planned, incremental changes that lead to their final solution. It cannot be said enough: do not underestimate the left. Leftist incremental cultural changes are by design, from day one.

Redistribution

Redistribution, otherwise know as RHS or *Robin Hood Syndrome*, is romantically portrayed as taking from the rich and giving to the poor (after Robin takes his cut, of course!). In reality, it is a systematic looting of all economic classes from the poor on up. The scam usually begins under the guise of needing to enact "necessary reforms" (otherwise known as punitive regulation, laws, and taxes), which results in the transfer of wealth from the private sector to the "public sector" for programs that *reportedly* serve the public at large. In actual practice, the majority of the collected loot is virtually stolen from the government kitty by leftists and their cronies before it reaches the proposed target. At the same time, public attention is redirected to a sideshow that directs a trickle of funds to the down and out and less fortunate—the very ones the left loves to tout as the most virtuous among us and yet they do everything to ensure they stay in their caste.

While we are on the subject of trickling, is it not interesting that any trickling of funds associated with redistribution is one trickle-down theory the left embraces? In true capitalistic trickle-down, the economic engine generates wealth that streams directly and indirectly to all. In true *leftist trickle-down* (the counterfeit version), the funds from the economic engine are confiscated by the government entity, thereby impeding the proper functioning of the economic engine, which in turn causes an economic downturn. After the confiscated funds are reduced by political thieves to resembling a stripped carcass, the remaining scraps are thrown out to the masses, which then trickle, better said drip, into an already anemic economy. So you see, leftists do believe in trickle-down theory; they just believe in their own special little version.

Now if you are one of those romantics who think that redistribution would be virtuous if only it was done as intended, I have a revelation for you: redistribution is immoral. If you are still in shock from the last statement and are reluctant to see the immorality of redistribution and need some moral support, let's quote a moral authority that the left in the western world loves to quote: Jesus (perhaps in other parts of the world, leftists love to quote Buddha or whoever the local populace looks to for spiritual guidance). Now, Jesus did say to give to the poor, but he never said to take from the rich (or anyone else for that matter) and give to the poor. He also said to do unto others as you would have them do unto you. Would you want your neighbor to take from you and give to another? I think not.

Of course, the favored primary method of redistribution is via taxes. And again, leftist subterfuge is behind the curtain, just as it is in everything the left does. Take the idea of progressive or graduated tax rates. The basic underlying principle relies on the idea that if the rich pay a higher tax rate than other classes, a higher rate can then be justified for the middle class. And some of you thought it was the other way around! Say, for example, that the rich pay 40 percent. Who then is the middle class to complain about 20, 25, or 30 percent? However, if the rich pay 20 percent, lefties would have to lower the middle class rate to keep alive their *class envy* argument.

And what about the poor who do not supposedly pay taxes, you ask? Through sales tax and taxes on corporations, the poor are paying a higher percentage than they ever realized. Even in the face of such overwhelming evidence, don't bother holding your breath for lefties to "get it." Lowering taxes is fatal to the scam.

Yet taxes are not the only way in which redistribution (by the way, a foundational communist value) happens. Remember, at this point in the game, leftist allies seeking funds have infiltrated most, if not all, sectors of society. Therefore, funds can be redistributed from anywhere to anywhere. Such redistribution is just as damaging as and sometimes even more infuriating than taxes. Once ensconced inside government entities, operatives direct funds and redistribute them from traditional programs to nontraditional agendas. The tactic supports a dual purpose. First, it depletes the traditional program of funds (such as public works). Second, money is distributed to leaders and cohorts in the cabal of constituencies.

The outcome for the leftist is pure ecstasy since multiple goals are accomplished. Depleting existing programs, which are necessary for a properly functioning society, causes degradation of services. This will typically occur in the areas of security (such as fire and police), public services (such as water or waste disposal), and infrastructure (such as roads). When these services are lacking or deficient, the taxpayers scream for resolution. The answer? More revenue is needed! Once the method for confiscation is enacted (taxes, fees, bonds, etc.), more money is available to fund the nonessential/political supporters of the left that created the mess in the first place!

And yet, just raiding the public coffers is not enough. The private sector is too vast of a pool of wealth to pass up for these drooling power freaks. To go after that piece of the pie, bogus directives, laws, regulations, and cases are brought to bear for the sole purpose of defrauding individuals or corporations and to swell the coffers of the liberal causes.

The creativity of the left opens up a potpourri of ways to confiscate OPM (a.k.a. *Other Peoples' Money*). Legislators will target a private sector entity, which they want to destroy, that either a) does not support their party, b) supports the opposition, or c) just so happens to be a convenient bystander. Legislation will be passed to aid and abet the transfer of funds from the opposition's support constituency to one of their own, who in turn pass on campaign contributions in what is yet another endless, vicious cycle. In nothing more than a casual wink, leftist administrations, legislatures, bureaucrats, and judges work hand in hand to redistribute funds and destroy society.

And yet the fraud does not end there. Advocacy groups, usually under the banner of civil liberties, will sue governments and corporations for the unexpressed purpose to enable a legal exchange of funds from the government or corporation to the advocacy group. It is entirely possible that all participating parties are in on the scam: the plaintiff, the defendant, and the judge, the goal all along being to transfer money legally to the leftist cause so they can move their agenda forward and sue again! Some are so good at this tactic, no action is necessary. Just threaten a target with potential action and money will be transferred from the target's coffers to the leftist pillowcase in an electronic transaction minute. The process becomes even easier if leftist agents have already infiltrated the target entity. If they are not already doing their part to redirect funding to their favorite pet projects, claiming pressure from legal threats can make redistribution easier to justify for the moles in the mix. If you ever wonder how leftist groups find funding, check out their sources: follow the money. You may be surprised by some old money names that are funding contemporary radical groups.

This maddening cycle will repeat itself endlessly until the golden goose keels over, satisfying another goal of the left—economic deconstruction. By supporting the left's favored constituencies, redistribution allows them greater ability to market their ideas, confiscate more funds, and destroy the economic engine. Redistribution is a typical, socialist sleight of hand—nothing more than a middle man inserting himself to force a transaction that will benefit the middle man more than any of the other participants. More importantly, redistribution is never about any measure of equalization in any shape or form. The impetus behind redistribution is that, to Lefty, material wealth offers independence, and in the leftist paradise, any form of independence must be abolished. Redistribution ingeniously provides a method to erode and eradicate that pesky notion of independence.

Regulatory Sprawl

Admittedly, bureaucracy is not necessarily a creation of the left, but on its own merits it innately contains a strong current of self-preservation and job security. But to the leftist operatives in the mix, any government process that is effective and beneficial must be "corrected." Not only must it become expansive to support leftist minions (as my father said many times, "Welfare is not for the poor, it is to provide jobs for the politicians' families and friends"), but it also must be "improved" until it meets leftist standards. And because of the end leftists have in mind, every time liberals "improve" something, it gets worse!

Any frustration experienced by the average citizen foreshadows the ultimate purpose of building the bureaucracy: to build the nanny state to the point where government completely controls every aspect of your life. The bigger and more intrusive government is, the greater control it has over the citizenry. When the government has programs for someone who needs a job, loses a job, has children, needs health services, needs a loan, needs psychological counseling, and on and on, why would one ever need to rely on private enterprise or their fellow man? Exactly! *The socialist ideal is not to make us one society, with people who rely on each other, but to separate us from one another to the point where the mother or father state becomes our only comfort.*

Factionalization

The left loves to rave about equality, but in truth they want and need to keep groups separate and unequal. *Always remember, the left is never about equality for all, only about superiority for leftists.* The main theme in factionalization is to keep people separated into groups because groups are easier to control, manipulate, and influence. Lefty works hard to keep reminding them that they are distinct from other sectors of society and thus, require special treatment; to repeatedly tell them in a mantra-like fashion that they are victims; to constantly inform them that they need to be protected from the "other" factions of society that "have and will" take advantage of them; but most of all, to reassure the group that they need the protection of Lefty.

Factionalization is the whole purpose behind bilingual education. Keeping immigrants separated from the mainstream allows the left to tailor and direct the socialist message to the immigrant group. If there is anything that the left is a master at, besides deceit, it is the marketing and selling of deceit. Naively, the political right stands around believing that the principles they stand on speak for themselves. That would be nice if it were true, but it is not. Unfortunately, we live in a world where ignorance is reborn every spring. If principles were universally self-evident, the left would never have a chance. But the fact is, they are not—especially when the left is constantly supplanting the truth with their counterfeit notions. Take, for example, the seemingly perennial story of people picking wild mushrooms, ingesting them, and then dying from mushroom poisoning. The story is in the news often enough, and yet it happens time and time again. One would think that we would learn after a few thousand years, but alas, that is not the case. We must accept the fact that although truth may be universal, truth is not universally known. People, old and young, must be constantly educated. The left inherently grasps this concept, while the right, sadly, apparently does not.

Unions are another example where factionalization facilitates controlling large groups of the populations. The average union worker is simply interested in the best wage and benefits for him or herself and his or her family. Naturally, they look to union leadership for guidance and direction. After all, the leadership of most groups is typically comprised of members who understand the other members' concerns. It is the job of the leadership to look out for that group's best interest and research issues that the average member does not have the time or the desire to research. Enter stage left: with union leadership in their pocket, the left is granted access to the membership audience via mailing lists and the membership's pockets via dues. The left is then in a prime position to tailor a message to a virtually captive audience: one man's "member education" is another man's indoctrination.

Think of it: union members are forced to pay union dues, which amount to private enterprise taxation, to fund propaganda directed right back at themselves! One has to give the left credit for being masterfully deceiving. Oh, and by the way, any opposition within the ranks to the self-sponsored propaganda, and the legal pick pocketing, is dealt with, leftist style.

Factionalizing is the same game as class warfare (historically know as *envy*, one of the seven deadly sins). This is the very reason why the "rich" are often a target of the left. They are always a minority of any society and are too convenient of a scapegoat for socialists to pass up. The irony is that there are rich socialists who will deride the rich for being rich. This just goes to show that socialists have the ability to say anything at any time, while excluding their own circumstances. They are used to having their cake and eating it too. This may explain their inability to fiscally manage anything well.

Lefty knows that manipulation of segmented political constituencies can wield tremendous power in close contests. Therefore, they like to subdivide the nation into groups and speak to them in terms of their special rights and special needs. That way, the left, by appearing to be the sole acknowledger of the special groups, by default becomes the savior. To further ensure allegiance, the left will claim they will fight for what is commonly perceived to be a vulnerable group, like women and children—groups to which they have granted automatic victim status. The political right, on the other hand, naturally opposes the left. Therefore, the twisted logic follows that the political right must also be against women and children. Likewise, when the right insults the left, the left records an implied insult against all women and children!

If we are all equal and supposed to be treated the same, why do they segment groups in society and assign special rights to them? The answer is obvious to anyone who understands Lefty: it serves the purpose of pitting everyone against everyone. This type of fragmentation is replicated enough times until the understanding is that the political right is against all groups: minorities, women, children, poor, middle class, working-class ... anyone left? Oh yeah, the rich!

Persecution Lite

Nothing more than political character assassination, the practice of soft persecution calls for legally hounding a political enemy until a) the target virtually withdraws from the fight or b) some charges are found that will stick. All is done because the political target holds a different belief. The process is never brief (as intended) and is a prime example of psychological warfare. With charges hanging over one's head, one is sidetracked from offense and may be reluctant to cause any more waves until one's name is cleared. If baseless legal charges do not hold water, then the process of receiving constant negative press may exact enough damage on the opponent(s). Elected leftist attorneys have been known to frivolously open up the taxpayer coffers to go after political enemies or "noncompliant" individuals, only to be forced to drop the case later on.

With accomplices in the media, the legislature, and the judiciary, the task is made easier by biased reporting, legislation, and judgments thrown at the target. This is the impetus behind such great-sounding initiatives like "campaign finance reform." The "reform" is put in place to facilitate prosecution of political enemies of the left. It has a second benefit of putting trepidation and fear into the average citizen who is considering running for office. Campaign Finance Reform would better be labeled Candidate Intimidation and Elimination Act.

Another ruse employed when hounding opponents: fascists love to claim underperformance. When dealing with such a leftist, understand that there is virtually no performance will ever be good enough, no matter what. If the leftist is in power, however, good enough or not, no mention of incompetence is ever made by the sycophantic press. However, when targeting the right, every fault will be magnified to disgust the public. In turn, in a virtual march to the steps of government, the leftist antagonists claim to have a mandate for change. Not the type of change that would ensure that outcomes would improve the next time around. Leftists do not want to solve problems; they want to perpetuate them, even when they are in power. The only change leftists want is a change that can further their aims.

Naturally, because of their nature, when the left is in power, the management of public affairs will typically be worse, first, because their illogic makes government worse, and second, because they do not want it fixed. A broken system gives them an issue to complain about when the opposition is in power. As a matter of fact, leftist governments, after a defeat in the polls, may leave the incoming opposition with dysfunctional government agencies that were ruined by the leftist regime itself. The result, leftist figureheads leave a lot of their cronies behind to sabotage the new incoming government; these cronies, in turn, then sabotage and work secretly against the new administration. Then, get ready for this, the ousted leftist power claims the same government agencies are mismanaged!

Socialists also like to couple the charge of underperformance with the tactic of demanding resignation, and again, understand, it does not matter the reason because, in any event, reason is never at play. The goal is not to ensure that the office is held by a person of reasonable sensibilities. No, the goal is to extract one more casualty in the political battle, then, once the person resigns, they fight over the replacement. Do this enough and there will not be many volunteers left to take the future positions. The media plays a role by spotlighting every potential nominee in such a way that sends the message: "Do you truly want to subject yourself, your family, and your friends to our national exam?" When potential candidates see nominees go from obscurity to being portrayed as the next potential mass murderer, no person in their right mind would want to jump in the game. Only a true patriot, knowing the potential outcome, would offer up his life for such a gauntlet—the very person the left does not want in this position. So, working hand in hand, leftists do their best to discourage participation.

Lest we forget, another facet to soft persecution: intimidation. As the left becomes more entrenched in the seats of power and feels freer to express their views, they become more open about who they are. Political leaders may send threatening letters or make threatening overtones to business leaders. Radical groups will send open threats to news outlets. Advocacy groups will barrage organizations with a letter campaign. If the target is already infiltrated with a leftist sympathizer who is a key decision maker, *fait accompli*: the target will accommodate the fellow fascists' demand, publicly claiming some ridiculous reason for "caving in." But once again, the reason does not matter.

To most, the fact that political leftists are intimidating business leaders or news organizations probably means nothing. But in fact, it is the mark of a major paradigm shift. Having been successful in defeating their political rivals, Lefty now sets his sights on private citizens. Once the left culls through the strata of one class and emerges victorious, they then go after the next target, and then the next, and then the next … until they arrive at your doorstep. We should all care about the millionaire between them and us. The left loves to tell us that the rich are oppressing the poor and middle classes, but the truth is that the rich are actually oppressing the left from targeting the rest of us! By the way, this tactic makes it easy to spot the impostor. Whenever they deride the wealthy or a corporation—basically anything that they want to destroy—you can be sure they are leftists (funny how wealthy leftists are never labeled as oppressive!).

Another tangential offshoot of legal persecution, deflection, is a favorite tool of leftists with subpoena power. The purposes are multifold. One, negative attention is cast on, and associated with, the opposition. Two, negative attention is cast away from the shenanigans of the current leftist powers. Three, the opposition is put on defense and is kept occupied fighting the latest round of charges rather than fighting the aforementioned shenanigans. It also has a chilling effect on those who might speak out otherwise; who wants to end up with a subpoena? Be wary of politicians promising and promoting investigation after investigation. Chances are that what they are doing is much worse than what the target of the "investigation" ever did.

Oppositional Aid and Comfort

Providing aid and comfort to the enemies of freedom is by far the one tactic that is very difficult to understand, or even detect, because in context, it defies logic. Take any free country in the world and you can be sure that there are leftists sprinkled throughout the government. For such individuals, the home country is the enemy! Therefore, as the twisted logic ensues, any person, organization, or state that is an enemy of the free country is a natural ally to the leftist, regardless of whether that entity's goals and the leftist's goal are in tune with each other. The fact that the entity is also in favor of chipping away at the foundation of the free state is good enough for the leftist.

This is the part that defies logical sense: even though the leftist has benefited from the freedoms of the home country, its continued existence prevents the realization of the leftist's dreamy existence: total power and control. In their heart of hearts, leftists are *leftists*. With such individuals, power and control is not just the ultimate aphrodisiac, it is the only aphrodisiac.

Such is the insane paradox that socialists engage in: allowing the destruction of the country in which they live, while holding on to the idea that they themselves will rise out of the ashes and grab the reigns. Progressives believe that tyranny rises out of destruction, and that for every blow at the foundation of a republic, they are one step closer to the overthrow of the system. This is why it is imperative for them to embolden, abet, and support the enemies of that republic *without* blowing their own cover. To the average observer, not realizing what is actually happening, the modus operandi is unthinkable.

For example, a national policy may be in place that prohibits natural resource recovery under the guise of protecting the environment, yet national security and an entire economy is allowed to tank, regardless; the public is incessantly told how much future generations will pay for tax cuts or wars, yet never is the public apprised of the explosive costs of the left's ruinous social programs; sanctioned and unsanctioned diplomatic missions are made to foreign governments and organizations that support tyranny and terrorism, under the guise of starting a "conversation" (the scheming that occurs on these junkets can only be imagined); restrictive firearms laws are passed under the guise of preventing crimes, the result being the opposite.

Everything Lefty does is counterintuitive. Average freedom-loving individuals may believe that such degenerates are just like them and working in their own "special" way for the public good. Do not be fooled. They are salivating in the quest for power, and their intentions are maniacal from the get go. For example, just look at the regions in the world where firearms are most restricted. The populace is either subjected to an empowered criminal class or an empowered police state. Those areas around the globe where self-defense is most restrictive, or even punitive, have the highest crime rate and the greatest number of residents in jail. But these facts are kept out of any leftist diatribe. From the left's perspective, citizens shouldn't have firearms because citizens who can defend themselves are not dependent on the government for their personal protection—and therein lays the issue.

Dependence on a central authority is the strata on which the foundation of socialism rests. Therefore, the conclusion is that any *independence* must be bad, regardless of any reasoning offered, because it conflicts with Marxist propaganda. As stated before, lack of dependence is the primary reason why leftists openly target the rich, and believe it or not, more than having access to their wealth, they want their independence abolished! Independence is the antimatter to the leftist dream of power and control. Therefore, anything that promotes independence, be it wealth, firearms, speech, private property, or otherwise must be *incrementally* limited until it can be done away with completely.

The Final Curtain

Once Lefty acquires sufficient control of society's levers, the plan goes into overdrive. From outright voter fraud and voter intimidation, bogus opinion polls and studies, raising taxes and fees, purposely bloating entitlements and increasing debt, to legal and legislative persecution, the left engages in multiple forms of "legal" violence that precede the last and final stage of Lefty's trek: takeover.

Once a society has reached this stage, it is prepped and ready for extinction. Although violent coups have overthrown governments in a matter of days, many have failed. Violence, a great catalyst for takeover, is a highly risky venture. The preferred method is a slow death, where there is less risk for the leftist. If a little violence in the end will finish off the remaining freedoms and has a modicum of risk, Lefty may take the plunge. In the end, whatever the method, whether by a quick or slow death, once the cultural castle is successfully stormed, the operation is completed; releasing its last assurance, the candle of freedom smolders in the darkness.

Most of these tactics may seem hard to believe, but one must understand that many a society in history has failed to believe that they were even under attack. Even more so, an attack from within is much less suspected or detected. Caveat civis! The closer Lefty gets to his goal, the more giddy, rabid, and foaming at the mouth he becomes. Delirious with the thrill of expectation, his plans become more transparent. Those who are wise will note that invariably, Lefty unwittingly telegraphs the next phase in his plan.

Yet, as free republics slumber, the left prepares to invade and conquer. While those on the right are focused on the current fight du jour (and unfortunately, usually in a defensive stance), the left is already thinking ten moves ahead and has most likely already laid out the plan to manufacture steps one through nine.

It is frustrating to watch, as those on the right seem to have a penchant for underestimating the left. It is likely rooted in the fact that leftist ideas are utter nonsense and their ultimate aims contradict the principles of freedom. This is truly a grave mistake. Never, ever underestimate the left or the depths to which they are willing to sink and take the rest of us with them.

The Players

"The world is a dangerous place to live—not because of the people who are evil but because of the people who don't do anything about it."
—Albert Einstein

Nothing is perfect in life—not for the political right nor for the political left. This can be a good thing. Just as the left exploits human nature to further their agenda, the uncertainty and imperfection of human nature may be that which impedes leftward progress. If all of the tactics discussed so far yielded full impact every time, Lefty's walk to the throne of power would be an easy ride. But lo and behold, there is an unpredictable element within human nature that distinguishes us from animals and robots: we have opinions. We are the outcome of a collage of life experiences and influences that make every human being truly unique. Opinions can bind us together or separate us.

And so it is with the left, which, like any political body, is comprised of opinionated entities and is therefore not monolithic. Nor are all factions working in perfect, harmonious concert, even though it may seem that way. On the contrary, the left consists of several major and minor factions, each struggling for the mantle of power, each wanting to push their pet agenda to the forefront. Where there are some factions wanting to force their agenda immediately, there are others that call for patience. And to add to the mix, there are those factions who reluctantly give lip service to their fellow fascist travelers, waiting for the day when they can grab the mantle of power and eliminate those with whom they have been dependently, yet reluctantly, yoked. It cannot be overstressed: being a leftist is a difficult life. This may offer a partial explanation of their insane rants and beliefs. The paranoia and self-imposed psychological torture that occurs must be torment, knowing that your ally today might be your mark tomorrow, or worse: you may end up being your ally's mark.

Yet to Lefty, the obsession for power is the sum of all that matters. Consequently, the recurrent psychological damage resulting from such an insane existence has to be suppressed for the sake of temporal cooperation. For in the interval, between the lust for power and its final acquisition, sheer numbers are needed for progress. Until that day arrives, the quest is on to see who grabs the mantle of power first. Until then, the fractious coalition members must continue to wake up in the morning and ask themselves: "What would Marx do? Or Lenin, or …" As a comfort to the tortured souls, the faithful of the contentious tribes can find solace in the notion that they all share a common, obsessive desire to have power and control over the rest of us—our lives, our activity, our words, and our very thoughts.

With that in mind, let us explore the various factions of the left, and how in the end, their seemingly harmonious bonds are scuttled when the time is ripe.

The Power Left

The power left is the faction that simply wants power. Although money is a necessary and desired component of this club, it is not the ultimate desire. The ultimate desire is the power to dominate a country, a region, and even the world, if possible. Understandably, these rogues are usually the most insecure and insane of all types and are therefore the most dangerous. As we have discussed before, their desire to rule can usually be traced to their own psychotic insecurities. Famous members in this club would include members of the "Twentieth-century Dictator Club" such as Mao, Stalin, and Hitler.

Now, just because a republic or democracy is devoid of any sitting dictator, do not assume that there are not any wannabes lurking in the shadows. Just as the sky is blue, you can be sure that there are those who walk in freedom's light and yet covet overarching power. No one knows who they are, and for that matter, even their fellow comrades may not know who they are. They are Manchurian candidates of their own making, waiting to leap on the stage when the time is ripe, ready to seize the power they crave and lust.

These are the true maniacal ones. Living in their own concocted world, they dream of one day having power over all life and death. They usually have a laundry list of psychoses that went undetected until it was too late. Even with their psychological deficiencies, in a manner that defies common sense, they may see themselves as a god or a messiah. Think of the great pharaohs, emperors, and kings of history who were held as gods or godlike in their culture. It is easy to brush over the fact that this was just part of the fabric of a rudimentary culture. But it provokes several questions: Who created such a culture? What steps led up to the culture believing that the pharaoh was a god? Who implanted the seminal idea? Who nurtured the idea until it came to full acceptance? What tactics were used to blunt natural opposition? The idea of pharaoh as a god could not have just sprung up overnight. There was obviously an evolution of thought that morphed a human into a god (one evolution lesson that leftists do not want you to think about). One or more individuals had to seed and foster the notion until it came to fruition.

Interestingly, the lust for power has not changed since man has first walked the earth. And no matter how bright the future may be, this fact of life will not change. This is not meant to be a depressive statement, only a reminder that the scepter of power is pursued by deranged individuals and is a part of the game. We must condition ourselves to understand that such power ravens were not done away with in the last war or the last century. Yesterday's pharaoh is not a bygone relic but one of the original models. Today's power leftist is the same as yesterday's pharaoh. The labels have changed, but the themes are generally the same: power concentrated in the hands of one or a few individuals, at the expense of the many.

The Religious Left

The religious left is the making of three subcultures. In one subculture there exists the "all roads lead to heaven" crowd. They typically offer a message that there is a greater consciousness that awaits us all if we just listen to them and their "enlightened" message. They range from the sublime to the most radical, the most radical exerting the most control, such as cults. For example, when the membership of a cult swells to a critical mass, the "need" arises to move to a more "harmonious" environment, separated from the "disharmony" of the world. After such an edict, members are drawn to an earthly sequestered "paradise," in a communal setting that offers freedom from the cares of everyday life—at least that is the selling point.

What actually happens is that members trade a life in the everyday world for a life in a secluded one, full of brainwashing and mind control. The leader ("guru") turns out to be a self-styled dictator who could not sway a country into followership but had enough skill to sway a small collection of those who think the least of themselves. These insecure types are the perfect type for a cult leader, because they will blindly follow and lose themselves for the cause.

With that being said, isolation does not have to occur for successful *cult*ivation; insulating individuals completely from society is ideal, but not all cults end up in a sequestered environment. Some operate within the fabric of society, reinforcing doctrine through heavy doses of guilt and regular brainwashing sessions. Regardless of their implementation, under the guise of spirituality, religious leftists exhibit the qualities of the leftist ideal: one or few having power and control over the lives of others.

The second subculture is not really the product of religious beliefs but more of evolving social desires. In this leftist sect, one will find libertine notions and agendas looking to burrow inside traditional denominations. Then, once established as part of the congregation, they constantly and unrelentingly push liberal ideology on the original homesteaders. Their ultimate purpose is to force the adherents of traditional doctrine to take a more liberal standpoint on social mores. Once this is accomplished, the church-crashers then use the banner of religion to claim sanctification for their progressive social ideology.

For the most part, the targeted faiths are comprised of denominations or sects that have been infiltrated for the purpose of providing cover and acceptance to the *social left's* (discussed later) beliefs. Rather than accept the traditional teachings and preserve them for future generations, they seek to transform and overturn them to fit their version of morality. To sum it up, the social left uses a time-honored institution to transform a traditional religion into another bastion, supporter, and promoter of liberal thought. Think of it as a tailor-made religion to fit your lifestyle: believe it your way!

The third subculture is that of state-sanctioned religion. As with all leftist ideologies, it is nothing new. Many cultures have had state-sponsored religions that were used to oppress, influence, and control the masses. Fortunately, and not surprisingly, many have passed into history. In essence, this third type of subculture really boils down to the *power left* using religion as a vehicle.

In the leftist religious state, scripture interpretation is (conveniently) left up to one or a few. In turn, through the voice of one or a few, they instruct the adherents, willing or not, on how to behave and think. And because the leadership is represented as being "close" to the deity, questioning them can elicit charges of heresy and spiritual enmity—charges that may lead to a death sentence. Make no mistake, state-sanctioned religious radicalism is nothing more than tyranny draped in a priestly façade.

Opposing Faiths

The stark contrast between social leftists and power leftists in the religious realm raises the question: what happens when the two factions are operating in the same cultural space? The answer is found by inspecting their respective *modus operandi*. When *social* leftists infiltrate and subvert a religious body, the primary purpose is to expand the religious doctrine to include their liberal dogma. In contrast, when *power* leftists invade a religious body, the primary purpose is to bring about political Armageddon. For the power leftists in the religious arena, only one road leads to heaven or else! Disbelief in their brand of faith is punishable by death. For them, religion is a convenient vehicle to bring the free under their power and control. So when social leftists and power leftists collide, it is the social leftists who either yield or are exterminated. Why? Because it is a simple matter of one group with a killer instinct (power leftists) that easily bowls over another group with a pleasure instinct (social leftists).

The Social Left

In this faction one will find the race-mongers, the feminists (gender-mongers), and the determined self-abuse crowd: the sexual revolution crowd, the drug crowd, the abortionist crowd, and any other eclectic collection claiming victimhood and demanding some form of special legal status and compensation. These "movements" that begin as disguised promoters of simple tenets like equal treatment, privacy, and equality eventually become full-fledged assaults on society, so much so that their rabidity spills over into all facets of the public square.

Contrary to the notion that the easing of societal mores will make us more relaxed, less uptight, and more accepting, the opposite is actually true. All of these liberal, social ideologies are baseless in their propositions, destructive to society and individuals, addictive in nature, and promote a never-ending drive to societal deconstruction.

Race Mongers

The world over has a well-known history of unequal treatment of minorities in many societies. These are facts that cannot be escaped: racism has existed, does exist, and just like leftists, may always be in our midst. And just as there is a history of unequal treatment, there is also a history of legitimate movements to counteract the unfair disparity and to bring about equality for all. It is on the backs of these legitimate movements that the racial left enters the stage to springboard off of the hard-earned labor of past *legitimate* gains for the purpose of legitimizing the illegitimate racial left.

Their goal, as with all leftists, is not equality, but to have superiority and to enact retroactive punitive damages (e.g., "affirmative distraction"). Even worse, by modeling the adoption of legitimate tactics, racial leftists embolden other radical factions. The result is an outcome the original seekers of equality probably never foresaw: their progeny hijacking the movement to grab power and to exact punishment. This should come as no surprise since racial leftists are no different than any other leftist: they are psychologically damaged and seething with hatred. Retribution is in their DNA, even if the target is not the original offender. The only important outcome to them is that, in the end, someone else pays a price and they end up on top. As crazy as it may seem, race mongers in their core are leftists and therefore have a vested interest in perpetuating racism.

Serendipitously, these rabid racists are handed factors that play into their favor: a movement with legitimate concerns, actual victims, and unjustified inequality. Who can argue against it? And that is exactly the tactic they use to get what they want. Armed with bona fide arguments sans a bona fide cause, they approach legislators and judges with the appeal of righting historical wrongs (for the decision maker on the receiving end, decisions may be influenced by feelings of guilt just as much as the idea of being hailed as a liberator). After a few victories, coupled with some time and experience under their belt, racial leftists' requests turn into demands. Predictably, as the racial leftists float nearer to the mantle of power, mental degradation follows, to the point where every obstacle in their life is a product of racism. From that point on, anyone standing in their way is painted as a racist. The de facto standard line becomes thus: either completely accept them and their ideas or be labeled a racist!

This type of leftist miscreant loves to take the microphone and spread the destructive ideology to the target minority. The rant may sound something like this:

If you were born a minority, then you are automatically underprivileged. Did you know that? You are a victim born into an unfair world of oppression. Something is owed to you! You do not need to earn it, because it has been stolen from you. Besides, why bother even trying when the deck is stacked against you?

This kind of brainwashing has devastated minorities the world over. However sad it is to see, it must be even a thousand times more so to experience. How does this happen? Upon being informed of their status, target minorities look for political shelter under those who promise them a dreamy future. And who do they find waiting with open arms? Why, the friendly, local, leftist operative, of course. In return for ballot allegiance, the left exercises their dreamy ideas on these minorities. The results are devastating; their existence becomes a sub-cultural tailspin.

May it be a lesson to the rest of the world of what leftist principles do to a culture. By seeing what the left has done to minorities, we are given a glimpse of the leftist "paradise" that awaits us all. Visit any of the leftist enclaves the world over where the elected or appointed representation is left-leaning, places where the people elect leftists over and over or allow leftists to represent them and run their lives. These dark spots on the globe are where you will find misery, poverty, crime, and despair in perpetuity.

Beware of leftists promising … anything!

Radical Feminists

Akin to the racial left, only, radical feminists practice gender racism. In almost parallel fashion to the racial leftists, radical feminists springboard off of legitimate suffrage movements. Their goal is the same as it is with all leftists: superiority and retroactive punitive damages. They justify their cause based on the idea that the problems of the world are rooted in patriarchal hierarchy and that men are nothing more that idiotic buffoons (although, in all fairness, this type of behavior has been observed in nature, especially when beer is involved).

Now, given the life that some of the adherents to this philosophy have experienced, it is understandable why some feel they way they do. Seriously, some have truly been victimized. However, that does not translate to them being given carte blanche to redirect their anger at all of society. It would be just as ridiculous if, after being robbed by a foreigner, one forevermore considered all foreigners to be robbers. As is true with all leftists, they want society at large to soothe their psychological deficiencies by participating in and paying for their therapy (yet, being leftists, the root causes of the scarring can be difficult to discern). Consequently, one commonly finds oneself asking the enigmatic question: *so what do radical feminists really want?*

Radical feminists typically have other psychological aliases: lesbians and abortionists. Their antipathy toward men may explain the gravitation. Regardless of motivation, the feminist's ideal is a world devoid of men. But that being impossible, they crave the idea of a woman-ruled society, in the true sense of leftism. As sure as the sun is shining, do not rule out that some of the adherents to feminism are standard, garden variety closet dictators. Pity the poor radical feminist who lives a life frustrated by the fact that there are not many female leaders in history, much less dictators. To such a creature, the game is rigged and therefore explains why the world is off kilter—if only they could rule! Mussolini, move over!

Determined Self-Abusers

This crowd loves to rally around two central themes: 1) "It is my body and who is anyone to tell me what to do with it?" and 2) "What individuals do in private is no one else's concern." At face value, the propositions appeal to one's basic sense of personal freedom. However, as with all leftist propositions, they are appealing in message only and are ultimately destructive in practice. The self-abusers love to throw out lines like, "Prostitution is a victimless crime." You think so? Just survey law enforcement and social services who deal with prostitutes and they can tell you what a farce that old line is.

For example, those who favor the legal distribution of narcotics argue that individuals should be able to ingest what they please; after all, it is their own body. Historical proven fact: narcotics and their effects do not isolate themselves to the individual; they impact society at large. The Opium Wars still serve as one of the greatest examples of the effect of narcotics thrust upon a populace. As Chinese nationals strived for independence from British rule, the British purposely flooded the streets of China with opium. The impact was devastating. The British almost decimated a generation with one little poppy seed. The result: The Chinese were subdued and the British held on to power for decades more.[9]

What's more, at the turn of the last century, many drugs that are illegal today were legal, and some were even thought to be curative. However, after seeing the effects of such "cures," legislators moved quickly to stop the spread. Why? Because they saw the destructive effects on individuals and were aware of the devastating effect it could have on society. Drugs can actually transform a person, in a short manner of time, from a productive citizen to a lethargic addict. Just listen to the testimonies of addicts. Some will relate that it only took once, *just once*, and they were hooked and ruined for life.

None of this is news to core leftists. The Opium Wars proved that narcotics are an effective weapon of war that does not require the firing of a single shot. This is the real reason why narcotic distribution and legalization are always part of a leftist strategy. The tactic serves to demoralize, deconstruct, and enslave a culture and is yet just another weapon used in the war on liberty.

Abortion Merchants

When it comes to abortion providers, some are in the practice because it is, believe it or not, simply a business. For others, such as radical feminists, it is the right to tell men that they will do with their body (and the little person's body inside of their body) as they please; while for others, such as the "zero population" crowd, who view each new child as an environmental resource drain instead of a gift from the heavens, abortion is an eco-friendly practice.

9   http://www.wsu.edu:8080/~dee/ching/opium.htm

Now if one really thinks about it, abortion fits well in the leftist agenda: the power over life and death and the ability to ultimately control the lives of others. After all, the more control leftists have, the better they feel, even though leftists love to claim that they are for the "little guy." What leftists are shy to mention is the small print detailing that such protection is only granted to the "little guy" only after he/she has made it out of the womb (and even that is up for question).

This raises an important question: leftists talk up a great future for all, if and when lefties are given the reigns of power. However, if they snuff out the life of a child in the womb, where is that child's great future? How ironic that on one hand, Lefty will promise those who made it out of the womb a fantastic existence in a leftist paradise while at the same time he will wipe out those still in the womb, and to boot, wiping out their chance to partake in that extra-womb paradise. Abortionists can say all they want about the baby not being a person until it leaves the womb, but they cannot escape the fact that they are terminating a future. If that child were allowed to pass through the birth canal and live be to ninety-five, it would be called a person. Riddle me this: if leftists, without blinking, can take the life of an innocent child, how much sympathy do they have for you and yours?

Sexual Revolutionaries

Like narcotics, sex can be just as addicting and destructive. Because of this parallel nature, sexual revolutionaries are just as blinded by their obsession as one who is addicted to narcotics. Likewise, they disregard the lessons of history and have an equal disregard for the glaring facts of the present. Like a business enterprise, they desire access to new markets; like a religious cult, they desire access to new converts. Sexual revolutionaries want to be free to practice their behavior anywhere, anytime, with anyone or anything.

To this species of leftist, the moral pillars of society that have maintained cultural stability are nothing more than artificially constructed barriers. And so, blinded by their narcissistic desire, they refuse to see that the elimination of these pillars means the sinking of the foundation upon which they, along with the rest of the culture, are resting.

There are multiple agendas in this camp, one agenda lined up behind another, waiting in the wings to spring their special version of depravity on society, as the moral bar is lowered by the latest agenda du jour. And even though each agenda may not be aligned or even be supportive of one other, in typical leftist style, each one willingly or unwillingly enables another. The reasoning behind this support structure is quite logical: if one behavior that is considered immoral is legitimized, either by social changes or legal edict, then why can't mine be next? Where does one draw *the line,* and who determines where that line is placed? Seizing on the opportunity, these type of social leftists claim cultural leadership and take over virtual management of "the line." Once in command of "the line," it can be put anywhere they want it, regardless of where history, science, and society concur.

The process a culture goes through from healthy to hedonistic is a vicious cycle: social radical efforts are further fueled by cultural breakdown, which is a direct result of an initial putsch. Fortunately, society does not have to be replete with well-versed historians, scientists, and moralists to buffer their advances. There are some very obvious outcomes that occur when venturing into such "liberating" territory. The emotional and psychological damage aside, one of the greatest underplayed causes and effects of permissiveness, is the spread of disease, ranging from those that cause lifetime irritations to those that cause cancer and ultimately, death.

One of the most well known of these "liberating" diseases is AIDS. While some may say it is a curse of God, a mathematician may point out that it is a case of mathematical probability. Purveyors of promiscuity tend to have many more partners than the average bear, and therefore the likelihood of disease contraction and spread is multiplied. The law of probability is the primary reason why AIDS has spread so rapidly through some communities and not others. In the past, social leftists threatened that AIDS would overtake the world and that the whole world would be subject to the same curse. It never happened. Why? Biology, nature, and mathematical probability!

Question: Is society better off because of the "awareness" that the sexual revolution has brought? This so-called revolution is the major force behind the spread of diseases such as AIDS and is behind the tremendous cost to healthcare systems. These diseases impact other areas as well, such as research, where money is taken away from traditional research, thereby slowing the progress on cures where people have contracted a disease *not* necessarily due to personal behavior. On top of all that, the legal process is straddled with additional burdens—burdens brought on by the radical agenda's obsessive desire to promote or repeal legislation that supports or limits their radical agenda. Additionally, not satisfied with legislative action, social leftists attack traditional organizations that are a positive force in the communities they serve, simply because these organizations refuse to be infiltrated and influenced.

And after all that, social lefties have the gall to claim victimhood. As with all social leftists, this is just a ploy to have society pay for social lefties' actions. Marauding as victims, they use buzzwords such as "tolerance" and "diversity," also known as code words that signal a demand for unqualified acceptance of their practices. And any notion to the contrary is know as "hate."

There are too many people who, when confronted with proponents of the sexual revolution, are all too willing to pass over a discussion. One must never forget those social leftists are just as radical as *any* leftist. And lest we forget, in a contest between a radical and an indifferent person, the radical wins. Never forget as well, behind one agenda is another in the wings, watching and waiting, champing at the bit to walk in the same footsteps. The potential outcome is much worse than one might think. If a culture cannot stop social radicals from waving legal papers in their face, how can it stop religious radicals from waving a sword?

The common thread throughout all of the factions of the social left is that they believe that they deserve social support and promotion based on their status as opposed to being based on their contribution to society. Unashamedly, they push obsessively forward, ignoring the wisdom of old—that is, a society where positions that are held because of status, instead of knowledge and experience, will slowly begin to unravel. But that does not matter to such types, for to them, how inadequate they feel is up to society to rectify, regardless of the consequences. And, to add to the paradox, their satisfaction and contentment are unreachable goals due to of the aberrant psychological nature of a leftist!

Another by-product of the social left *unleashed* is the social disarray that eventually leads to tyranny. Or stated another way, when a society becomes socially liberal, it invites socially oppressive movements. When a society is in a cultural freefall, there are those who get lost in the social chaos and yearn for structure. Burned out on the nihilistic or hedonistic lifestyle, they turn to controlling movements. Some of these may find comfort and solace in even the cruelest of doctrines, for these doctrines offer a way out of the chaos. Those who once thought moving socially left leads to a libertine "free for all" learn in time that it leads to systematic oppression. This lurch socially leftward fools society into thinking it is on a trek to personal freedom, when in reality, it ends up in universal bondage.

The Secular Left

A special mention here is made for an offshoot of the social left: the secular left. These are not just the nonbelievers; these are the militant nonbelievers. Not only do they not believe in a spiritual realm, but they also want to wipe the concept entirely from the face of the earth. Whether it is their desire for power or personal affinities, religion draws a line that they want to erase. Eliminate religion and man becomes accountable to man, or even better, as far as they are concerned, there is no accountability at all.

Removing religion from society can have a profound impact. If it is assumed that we are endowed with inalienable rights by a Creator—that is to say, rights that cannot be removed by the state—then the state is automatically impaired in its exercise of power and control. Accordingly, because those rights come from a superior Creator, those ordained rights cannot be infringed upon or taken away by the state.

The secular left's solution: take religion from the picture, and a vacuum appears that the tyrannical state is more than eager to fill. Thus, with the elimination of God from the equation, the fight rests between the state and the citizen to argue over who has what rights. Of course, in the leftist "paradise," it is the mother state that knows best and grants all privileges This elimination of God from the equation also serves another fancy craving of a leftist: it reinforces their belief that they are like a god and are therefore deserving of deification and worship.

This principle is so simple and yet the implications so great that one would think even a devout atheist would appreciate it. In a culture with a genuine religion, an atheist has inalienable rights that the state cannot seize; in a culture without religion, the atheists' rights are up for grabs too. History has proven that whenever God is replaced with the state, the masses are truly oppressed. Note to Karl Marx: it is not religion that is the opiate of the people; it is an oppressive government, emboldened by the absence of genuine religion, that is the opiate of the people.

Game Over

While all the factions revel in the advancement of their special agenda, the *power left* is ever plodding, quietly confident that none of the factions, save their own, will ever realize their ultimate aims. That is because in the very end, it is the *power left* that ends up in charge of the game. Of course, the *power left* will use the other factions along the way, casting a wink here and there, aiding and abetting the other factions' pet agendas. The treachery is done, knowing and understanding all along that collusion is a price to be paid in order to advance in the game. Once victory is achieved, however, and the other factions' usefulness expires, they too become subject to the same oppression as the rest of society.

After all, it is a practical matter, or as the saying goes, "It's a business decision, you understand ..." Because the *power left* requires a society that works as directed, libertine notions that exist in the *social left* disrupt order and must be put asunder. Similarly, religious themes that contradict or surpass the state's authority must be eradicated. Thus, in the end, the *power left*, in the form of a tyrannical state, becomes the one and only faction. No more positioning, nor more strategizing, only the sound of silence. Game over.

Paradise Lost

"What has been will be again, what has been done will be done again; there is nothing new under the sun."
—Solomon (c. 1000 BC)

History shows us that all the great leftist paradises promised throughout time exist only in speeches, books, and dreams. Because in reality, the great leftist movements of the past have left the cultures they infected in a devastated state—some even to the point of extinction. And yet there are those who say, "If only they would have done this ..." or "the mistake was ..." The mistake, or whatever excuse is employed, was never a matter of any form of logistics. The mistake was and is believing over and over again in the same failed ideology in the first place.

But let us suppose, that is to *suspend disbelief* for a brief moment, that these leftist agitators really believe what they are saying and that what they are saying is actually possible, that heaven can truly be had on earth and that a human paradise is within our grasp. Pushing aside immediate thoughts of an apparent psychosis and a disregard for all of history, let us explore the various aspects of such a wonderland.

Political Paradise

In the leftist political paradise, the state overarches all aspects of life. All are harmoniously intertwined and contentedly subject to the leftist architecture. All are part of the one, and the one is part of the all. Every individual works in harmony for the benefit of the entire cultural body. In this paradise, individuals look past their own needs and work toward those needs that will satisfy the whole. All are living and contributing to one great, harmonious collaboration.

However, somehow instinctively, Lefty knows that within the body of comrades, the universal desire to share does not exist. Therefore there needs to be an overall arbiter, but not just a mere discussion leader. This *uber* arbiter needs to have the power to overcome the tendencies of all the fellow reluctant philanthropists. This notion, in turn, gives birth to the concept of a central authority, comprised of individuals from the same population it governs. Funny, it is naturally assumed that the selected individuals will act appropriately in all matters even though they come from the same pool of reluctant philanthropists for whom a central controller is supposedly needed! But such trifling details do not matter to leftist ideologues. Besides, leftist wisdom teaches that appointed overseers are just like everyone else and yet at the same time *better* than everyone else.

As we return back to earth to observe socialism in actual practice, one learns that the political structure is actually comprised of an overbearing matriarchal or patriarchal state (take your pick, it does not matter). This mother or father state eventually becomes the primo director of all, coordinating all activity, suppressing all potential opposition to the system, and indoctrinating the masses to fully submit to a central authority. Order is maintained by force through such favored vehicles such as intimidation, persecution, starvation, and outright murder. Sound heavenly?

How is this so? Alas, the nature of man is suspiciously absent from the calculation of this manmade paradise, and it is done so purposely. That is because with the injection of human nature, also known as reality, the storyline breaks down. Leftists well understand the harmonics of human nature; after all, they are masters at manipulating it. They know full well that their paradise is a scam and is unachievable. Likewise, they do not care that it is nothing more than pure fantasy and that it will leave the culture in shambles. All that matters to them is that they control everything, shambled fantasy and all.

Economic Paradise

In the economic paradise of the left, one lives by the leftist golden rule: *from each according to his ability, to each according to his need*. Following through with this assumption, everyone works at his or her talent for the welfare of all. The doctor and the gravedigger work side by side for the sum benefit of the masses. Both receive relatively the same pay because, after all, they both offer a needed service to society. It does not matter that the schooling they had to attend or the daily pressures they have to endure are drastically different. It only matters that they use their talent to perform their compulsory duty for their fellow comrades.

In the socialist nirvana of the leftist state, education, healthcare, and employment are universally guaranteed. The state ensures that all are cared for from the time individuals take their first breath until the time they release their last. There are no economic worries for the individual, for the benevolent state, run by "concerned" comrades, is watching over all.

Hmmm ... first, one is to believe that there will be a government that is ready and willing to provide all economic benefits without question or any strings attached—a government that will provide a service of high quality and be as efficient as a private enterprise (ha!). One must believe in a government made up of administrators who will hold sway over everyone's economic fate and yet always act appropriately ... Hmmm.

Years ago I met a woman who had fled (note *fled*, not *left*) from communist Poland, one of the many "socialist paradises" contained within the former Soviet Bloc. She recounted how in Poland there were virtually no homeless people, the streets were always clean, virtually everyone had employment, and everyone had access to healthcare. Wow, sounded like heaven. So why did she leave?

She explained that other than minor hindrances like secret police and the like, no one really had the *freedom* to be homeless, for the state would find a place for everyone or else. The streets were clean because the state would make sure they were cleaned or else. Everyone had a job, so much so that several people would do the job of one person (another explanation for clean streets) or else. Incidentally, because there were realistically only a few hours of work per person each day, the greater part of the day was unproductive. Subsequently, all who did the job of one person would virtually share the pay of one person as well.

Yet the wonders of the incredible shrinking economic machine didn't stop there. She also described how one would stand in line for hours at the grocery store, *yes for hours*, just to receive a limited, sometimes rationed, supply of substandard goods. And not just store items were in ration mode: people typically waited for years just for a telephone line or an apartment (an apartment!). Oh, and lest we forget the jewel in the crown, healthcare. Sure, healthcare was available to all—whatever *was* available. Just like the grocery store, one could wait for hours to see the doctor and then, when the patient finally got to see the doctor, chances were that the equipment, materials, or medicines to treat the patient properly were not available.

Funny thing, the daily game of survival was a bit different if one happened to be an official of the communist party; funny thing, they somehow received preferential treatment. Just think, the whole communist promise to break the monopoly of bourgeois class was true after all—well, in a sense. It seems that the proletariat, the supposed benefactors of the socialist paradise, missed the fine print explaining how the "oppressive" bourgeois class was to be replaced by a much harsher oppressive political class!

Just as the law of gravity is no respecter of objects, the law of economics is no respecter of political ideology. Economic production and prosperity only increase when individuals have the freedom to act, an ethic that is missing from the leftist economic system. For the freedom to act is the author of incentive, the author of risk, and the author of progress. Because the socialist state has the power to tell someone where they will live and where they will work, which in turn determines many other aspects of one's life, individual incentive is squashed. Why struggle and work hard when your fate is in someone else's hands? For what? Why work harder than anyone else just to receive relatively the same pay? So not only does economic socialism fly in the face of the laws of economics, but it also flies in the face of the human nature.

The only reward in a leftist economy is that one is allowed to continue to breathe, and even that is not a guarantee. Combine this negative motivation with the ripple effect it creates, and such a culture will perform sub-perfunctorily, steering clear of being even *moderately* productive and prosperous, never mind ever reaching its potential.

Social Paradise

Here is what social leftists may daydream about:

> *Along every street in social suburbia lives a community of "families"—loosely defined collections of two or more individuals. There are street signs that read "Hate Watch," designating the neighborhood as a "hate" free area. All commune and share everything, and no desire is unmet. Children are raised by everyone, giving them full access to a range of diverse experiences, molding them into universally accepting, tolerant individuals.*

> *No moral boundaries exist. Extra-familial relations are fully accepted, as is recreational drug use. All are free to "expand" their mind and their horizon. Everyone has his or her own "branded" religion or belief system, free to believe what they want and when they want. Life is a ride without any hindrances.*

In this farcical dream, the idyllic village raises the child. In the actual social Valhalla leftists envision, the village people are too occupied with their own narcissistic selves to raise themselves, much less a child. It may all seem wonderful from the comfort of a viable, functioning society, but in practice, such ideology is devastating.

Just survey the history of the western world in the last few decades: little by little, taboos have been erased, traditional social norms have become viewed as antiquated, and deviations have been given mainstream clearance.

In what appears to be a series of events that have guided the cultural spaceship to a brave new world, it seems as though society has crash landed and found a planet that was once run by humans, now being run by apes. What was right and wrong decades earlier has become a matter of preference. How did this happen? It happened by sheer social incrementalism, that soft but persistent and obsessive nudging in the direction of the social left. In the process, with each step awry of the original ideal, society is opened up to new avenues, which lead to new problems, which then lead to, of course, "new solutions," which then add new problems, which in turn fuel the need for more "new solutions," and so on and so on.

In the libertine paradise envisioned by the social left, they leave out the *minor* details in their narcissistic quest for pleasure—minor details like diseases propagating rapidly through permissive societies; the stability and happiness that comes from having both a loving mother and a father as a consistent presence in one's life—a factor that is not only cherished by the receiver of such parenting but is eventually important to society as a whole. Instead of promoting proper parenting, Lefty likes to focus on education, school lunches, and day care. There is not a child in the world that would choose education, school lunch, and day care over a loving mother and father. But then again, promoting proper parenting is a strong antidote to leftist control—and that is contrarian to the goal! Lefty knows that just like diseases, family instability metastasizes throughout societies and leads to their eventual breakdown. And in the end, the ultimate curse of immorality is oppression, destruction, and death—all part of the takeover plan.

A visit to the ancient ruins of an extinct culture can sometimes reveal clues that support this argument. Exhibit A: at some point, the culture was flourishing and is now extinct. Exhibit B: at the height of the "good times," sexual immorality and its derivatives slowly engulfed the society. The correlation is clear: unbridled sexuality is a hallmark of a culture in decline. A culture immersed in hedonism is ready to be led into tyranny. This may be due to several possible factors: too much attention is paid to pleasure rather than the basics that keep a society viable, basics like familial stability and national defense; those burnt out by hedonism yearn for stability and naturally turn to or are coerced to turn to controlling movements; showing a propensity for giving up traditional values in one area, in this case personal morality, conditions a populace to give them up in another area: personal liberty.

Dream On

All the leftist visions of the past, present, and future have been, are, and will always be mere pipe dreams. History is replete with leftist agents attempting to craft utopias that fail and fail miserably. Nothing in history points to mankind as always having the best intentions. These political salesmen conveniently exclude human nature. As well, their entire logic (illogic rather) contradicts itself: if mankind were fully composed of the individuals they dream of, there would not be a need for police officers or correctional facilities or armies or *constitutions* or even the "utopian" government they love to promote.

The Challenge

"These are the times that try men's souls. The summer soldier and the sunshine patriot will, in this crisis, shrink from the service of their country, but he that stands it now, deserves the love and thanks of man and woman. Tyranny, like hell, is not easily conquered; yet we have this consolation with us, that the harder the conflict, the more glorious the triumph."
—Thomas Paine

As we stand at the dawn of a new millennium, there is a bolder style of leftist on the scene. That is not to say that leftists throughout history never reached such a stage. This stage is part of the cycle, one of many red flags appearing on the horizon. When leftists sense they are making traction, they consequently become bolder in deed and action and correspondingly become more open about their goals. This boldness is enabled further by a populace that seems to be easily conformed, which is in part due to the consistent leftist sowing (a.k.a. psychological conditioning) that has been going on for decades now.

Unlike their recent predecessors, contemporary leftists brazenly talk openly about what they want to do as their dupes and allies in the media continue to purposely redirect the focus to indeterminate issues. Thus, having become encouraged by their gains over the last few decades, today's leftists speak openly of overthrowing traditional institutions, subjugating democracies, wiping entire countries off the map, and the ultimate in leftist desires: world domination. In response, the world shrugs it shoulders, tunes out, and moves on.

The situation appears to be framed accordingly: on the left side of the conflict, there exists an illogical, immoral, obsessive opposition with long-term strategic plans making offensive moves. On the right side is a populace only partially tuned in, albeit well meaning, with no strategy and no offense. The only moves made by the right side are purely defensive moves, and typically only when made painfully aware of a clear threat.

The scenario may best be illustrated by the following. One night I became unusually engaged in watching an ice hockey game, where the players appeared to be around twelve years of age. I noticed that one team was consistently spending more time in the other team's home territory, thus having more chances to attempt to score, and thus scoring more goals. As the game progressed, it seemed as though the winning team became naturally offensive while the losing team became naturally defensive. I also noticed that with each successive goal by the winning team, the losing team appeared to become psychologically weakened to the point where it became easier for the winning team to score. In addition to the psychological toll, the physical stamina of the losing team's defense was drained prematurely from having to constantly fight off one offensive drive after another. Meanwhile, the winning team's defense had plenty of time to recover in preparation for a rare offensive drive from the losing team. In the midst of all this, I imagined the coach of the losing team thinking, *Where is the offense?*

I came away from that rink thinking how descriptive this was of the ideological war we are engaged in: on the left is an illogical, immoral, obsessive opposition that has been playing in our court for too long, while we on the right have assumed a defensive stance and have become, thanks in part to leftist conditioning, psychologically defensive. The question came to mind again: Where is the offense?

The Long Road Down

As we assess ourselves in the twenty-first century, are we closer to the ideals set forth by the great thinkers of history, or have we drifted farther away? Anyone's answer may depend on their point of view—and therein lays the problem. We have become a collection of viewpoints, so much so that morality has become a viewpoint—at least that is what we have been conditioned to believe. Up until now, you may believe that morality is a matter of one's personal view, only varying in perspective. But morality is a matter of right and wrong, dare I say, good and evil. The old leftist argument of "open up your mind" has been conveniently truncated. What they really mean to say is "open up your mind to leftist ideology and close it to all else." *Toleration*, the other mantra thrown at the culture all the time, is another convenient truncation. *The full intent is that we are supposed to tolerate leftist ideology in direct conflict with our own. In fact, the left will take toleration as far as we will tolerate, all the way up until our choice of toleration has been taken away.*

The progression of leftist "toleration" basically happens like this: First, we must tolerate their beliefs. Second, we must tolerate the practice of their beliefs. Third, we must tolerate the promotion of their beliefs. Fourth, we must tolerate legal protection of their beliefs. Fifth, we must tolerate attacks on our beliefs because they are disharmonious with their now tolerated, practiced, promoted, and legally protected beliefs. Sixth, we must tolerate legal limitations on the practice of our beliefs because they are in conflict with their tolerated, practiced, promoted, legally protected, and enlightening beliefs. Finally, our minds must be purged of our "outdated," antithetical beliefs or we ourselves must be purged because our beliefs are henceforth deemed intolerable!

The great fault for both sides of the political spectrum is to assume that the opposition is just like them. The left assumes that the right is just as cunning and devious as them. The leftist mindset is tainted by their outlook on life and does not allow them to believe otherwise. Likewise, on the right, the assumption is that leftists think just like those on the right: their intentions, although not always virtuous or perfect, are basically good and they truly do wish for the best outcome for all. This notion can be dispelled of quickly: when leftists defend and promote pornography (objectification of women and children), abortion (capitol punishment of the innocent), stay of executions for the guilty, early release and pardons for terrorists, revolving door justice for habitual criminals, limits on free speech, eradication of the right to bear arms (removal of self-protection), expansion of the welfare state, the proliferation of narcotics, rationed health care, ad nauseum—does it not raise the question: are these the actions of individuals who have the best intentions for all?

Those who are on the left have convinced some of us that the difference between us and them are degrees of understanding, thereby virtually diverting our attention while they methodically and quietly take over. We have been disarmed and muted, while they have been inoculated and emboldened. *As you and I have sat back and let them preach to us that we have no right to impose our morality on them, we failed to see that they were imposing their immorality on us!*

The bare truth is that we who believe in true liberty have capitulated (note, a defensive tactic) far too often in this war with the neo-political and neo-social engineers. Without an engaged opposition, the left is free to roll out its agenda through society. If you are one of those who think this ideological war is fictitious, then you are already defeated. To think of a liberal or a socialist as a harmless creature is the first mistake. Yes, they may seem harmless, but one must keep in mind the end game. Their counterparts in history have left the host societies in ruins and have led millions to their death, not to even mention the misery inflicted on the populace in the process.

When a society is accepting of leftist ideologies, such capitulation is akin to engagement with an alligator. Once society has compromised with the left, the death roll has begun. It is in this state that the socialist animal becomes bolder as it senses that victory is in sight. One must always keep in mind the end result of leftist hegemony: death, destruction, and desolation. The unhinged, seemingly harmless liberal of today is the potential death camp capo of tomorrow. It is vitally important that leftists are seen for the devastating, ugly end they will impose upon all, rather than their contemporary, seemingly innocuous façade.

In Germany in the early 1920's, the "Brown Shirts" (National Socialists or Nazis for short) were not taken seriously and were considered by some to be a bunch of overage boy scouts. Twenty years later, the world lay devastated as a result of this seemingly foolish bunch coming to power. Even Germany, the supposed benefactor of their new order, lay in ruins. Let history be your teacher and always keep this in the forefront of your mind. Leftism and all its tyrannical variations—liberalism, socialism, progressivism, National Socialism, Marxism, and communism—must be defeated on the spot. Otherwise, be assured that as you sleep, the left is conspiring to sweep your freedoms right out from under you and yours.

The rules of history dictate that the left is never extinguished; it can only be managed. There are times when the left controls and impacts mankind in a regional sense, such as in the failed regimes of the present and the past. In other times, the left has impacted mankind in a global sense, such as during world wars. To think that the left is extinguished at any point is a grave error, for it is then that the guard stands down, only to give the left another chance to start anew.

The notion of true liberty, that we have rights beyond the control of man, is what the left abhors the most. Thus, the foundations of liberty are under constant barrage from the left, because in their mind, if they can destroy the foundation, they can then do away with the principles of freedom and tailor society to fit their schemes. How do we counteract this assault? The key is this: if we are to defeat radical ideologies, we must first stop defeating ourselves. That begins with understanding that there is a clear and present danger and that we must be just as obsessive as our leftist counterparts and accordingly shedding our society of leftist ideologies and showing the proponents the door.

As Thomas Jefferson stated: "The price of freedom is eternal vigilance," and for emphasis, I would (humbly and respectfully) append: "... and the consistent repudiation of the left." But not only must we always fight the fight, guard the institutions, and protect the culture from the leftist assault, but we must also go on the offensive, standing on our valued freedoms, teaching the tenets of liberty to all generations. We must saturate our culture with the stalwart values of liberty with the same zeal the left has saturated it with their twisted ones. Only then will we be able to bring down the leftist house of cards, and keep it there.

As Teddy Roosevelt admonished, "Decisions determine destiny." So must we make decisions and actions to determine our destiny or leave it to the left to determine the destiny for all of us. Always remember: the left is always, always, always on the assault and will always strive for power and control over us and ours. We, therefore, must be just as diligent in our defense and advance of liberty for all.

> *"There will never be a really free and enlightened state until the state comes to recognize the individual as a higher and independent power, from which all its own power and authority are derived, and treats him accordingly."*

> **—Henry David Thoreau**